THE EVANGELICAL
CATECHISM

THE EVANGELICAL
CATECHISM

A New Translation for the
21st Century

TRANSLATED BY
FREDERICK R. TROST

THE
PILGRIM
PRESS
Cleveland

To my brothers, Theodore, David, Robert, and Jonathan,
who were nurtured on the catechism,
and to all the sisters and brothers
who are heirs of the "Evangelical tradition"
in the United Church of Christ

The Pilgrim Press
700 Prospect Avenue
Cleveland, Ohio 44115-1100
thepilgrimpress.com

Printed in the United States of America on acid-free paper

17   16   15   14   5   4   3   2

Library of Congress Cataloging-in-Publication Data

The evangelical catechism : a new translation for the 21st century / [translated by]
Frederick Trost.
     p.   cm.
  "The translation is based on several editions of 'The Evangelical Catechism' of
1929 as well as the earlier editions of 1892–1896 (when the catechism appeared both
in German and in English) and the original revision of the catechism of 1847, dating
from 1862. In this attempt to translate or restate 'The Evangelical Catechism' for the
twenty-first century, I have presented the various sections of the catechism in the order
in which they appeared in 1929 (when the last restatement was published). But I have
made one exception: the Ten Commandments. I have included the Commandments here
as Part I, as they originally appeared in the nineteenth-century editions of the catechism
and as they continue to appear in Luther's 'Small Catechism,' one of the three doctrinal
statements that remained particularly important to the Evangelical Synod of North
America" – Introd.
    ISBN 978-0-8298-1815-4 (alk. paper)
    1. Catechisms, German.   I. Trost, Frederick R.
BT1034.E9313 2009
230'.04624 – dc22   2009002981

Contents

Acknowledgments

I am grateful for the counsel of the following people, who have been extremely helpful at various stages in the preparation of this new translation of the catechism: Walter Brueggemann, Mark Burrows, Colleen Darling, Gabriel Fackre, Sr. Lorelei Fuchs, Reinhard Groscurth, Gerhard Koslowsky, M. Douglas Meeks, Robert Trost, Jonathan Trost, Sr. Mary David Walgenbach, Lowell Zuck, and my wife, Louise Herrman Trost. Their knowledge, wisdom, love for the Church and remarkable patience have been welcome gifts to me. I also wish to thank Michael Wilt and John Eagleson, whose editing skills, questions, and guidance in the preparation of this book have been both insightful and invaluable to me. The book's weaknesses and shortcomings are, of course, entirely my own.

Translator's Introduction
A Summons to Faithfulness

The summons to the Christian community in every generation is a summons to make the faith of the Church its own. At the outset of the twenty-first century, we are called, as our forebears were, to think, pray, explore, risk, and take to heart our vocation as witnesses to the Gospel. We are urged to accept the responsibility to live as ambassadors of the good news of God's radical and loving commitment to the world in Jesus Christ. We are invited to live in accord with the calling entrusted to us at the time of our baptism and to respond with discipleship to the Word proclaimed to the world by the prophets of old: the eternal Word that has taken form among us in Jesus of Nazareth. All of us, laity and clergy, old and young, women and men, parents and children, belong to the first few generations of Christians who have been summoned to proclaim the truth about God in proximity to the shadows of Auschwitz, beneath the crushing reality of Hiroshima and Nagasaki, and in a world that is filled with gods of many shapes and sizes. It is a world armed to the teeth.

The Preamble to the Constitution of the United Church of Christ calls upon communities of faith to become immersed in the truth about God and about ourselves. This ancient yet utterly modern truth is proclaimed by the apostles and martyrs of old, and the saints and sinners who have accompanied the Gospel of Christ through the ages. We are urged to listen to the voices of the Reformers of the sixteenth century, to their noble predecessors, and to the courageous ones who have sought to live by grace through faith in every generation. We are being called to live in discipleship as truly, boldly, humbly, and gladly as we can, both in moments of serenity and in times of chaos, the illogical and the absurd; to listen carefully (respectfully yet critically) to those who have come before us, to wrestle with them as necessary, to rejoice in their achievements, to take note of their failings, and to set sail across the tumultuous seas of the present, trusting in the providence, power, and abiding presence of the One who has promised: "I am with you always, even to the end of time."

We live our *faith,* however, not in the sixteenth or in the nineteenth but in the twenty-first century. We are summoned to *hope,* not at the edge of the Thirty Years War, but amid the challenges and complexities of the nuclear age. We hear the command to *love* God and neighbor, not as those struggling to make a living in the isolation of the Western frontier, but as part of a fast-moving and ever-changing society. Yet, is not our vocation as Christians the same today as yesterday? Will it not be the same tomorrow? Are we not being called daily to embrace the "new life" that is God's gift to us in Jesus Christ? Are we not, like our forebears, being summoned with the dawn of each morning to an awareness not only of the beauty of the earth but to the tears of God that flow in a flood across the world that has been shaped, despite every contradiction, by the grace of our Creator?

We are not unlike those who have come before us in the Christian faith. Like them, we have been called as witnesses, not just to any news, but to the good news, the "glad tidings of great joy" of which the angels sing, even in the depths of night.

The Scriptures proclaim and the sacraments embody the fact that God is in love with us all. It is the divine intention that we live gratefully in this world, actively facing the contradictions, injustices, cruelties, and needs that deny the new life given to us in Christ. Are these things not true? Those who professed the Christian faith before we were born shared a glimpse of this, did they not? Like us, they knew the imperfections and temptations of life. Or do we imagine this? Surely, they had a profound awareness of the depth of human sin. But in the midst of that reality, they were in their best moments able to proclaim with power and eloquence their trust in the grace of God.

The Evangelical Catechism is evidence of sound teaching in the Church. It presents a faith worthy of emulation — not faith easily tossed aside or planted in the rocky soil of fragile, questionable, shallow opinion, but faith anchored in the fertile ground of deep, joyous, hopeful conviction. We shall each, of course, have to work out our own salvation. As we try to do so, the footsteps of our immigrant forebears, shapers of the Evangelical tradition in the United Church of Christ, are worthy of exploration. They came from Germany and Switzerland in the 1830s and 1840s, making their way to Missouri, Illinois, and other states, places they sometimes referred to as *der Busch,* or "the wilderness." The little book they composed is not a compilation of profound theological knowledge. It is rather a piece of evidence that, at a certain point in time and at a certain place in history, there were those who sought, in plain, straightforward ways, to bear witness as best they could to the faith, hope, and love of their mothers and fathers, and at the same time to their own beliefs.

We are living at a different time and place, yet we bear the same responsibility they did. We are beckoned to the same vocation they had. We are being called to proclaim the same Gospel and the same hope, and not in soft, sentimental, or half-hearted ways but with depth and conviction. After all, the faith of the Church is a response not to a murmur but to a demand! As Georges Bernanos put it decades ago, the Church is called to live as "the salt of the earth, not the honey," always kneeling at the foot of the cross and remembering that "the prayer of the morning will determine the day." Humility and intelligence require that we attempt to do this while remaining aware that we owe a great debt to the witness of previous generations. Through the fire and smoke, the haze and indifference of our time, we are urged to behold that bent finger of John the Baptist pointing in the direction of the crucifixion. We are urged to recognize the presence among us of our crucified and risen Lord.

While the Evangelical Church Society of the West, which crafted the catechism in the nineteenth century, and the Evangelical Synod of North America, which brought the catechism into the twentieth century, were respectful of the teachings of the Protestant Reformation, pastors and congregations did not believe they should reside in the past, just as we do not wish to live there. They knew they had an obligation to make the faith of the Church their own, that is, to think through the faith they confessed prayerfully and to respond to the movement of the Holy Spirit that was urging them into the future. There were times of resistance, but they continued to press on. In the Evangelical tradition, this meant listening to the Church fathers and mothers, in particular the voices of the great Reformers: Martin Luther, Ulrich Zwingli, John Calvin, Philipp Melanchthon, Johann Brenz, and others. It meant paying attention to the passionate tradition of pietism that had helped shape their faith. Above all, it meant listening to the biblical story and attempting to shape the Christian life by its grace and power.

Where loyalty to their understanding of the Holy Scriptures and the pietistic urging of conscience caused them to differ with one or more of the great doctrinal standards of the Reformation (the Augsburg Confession, Luther's *Small Catechism,* and the *Heidelberg Catechism*), they insisted that the scriptural witness of the apostles and the prophets, the evangelists and the martyrs, speaks the definitive, abiding word. They pointed, as did John the Baptist, to the eternal Word of God. There is no doubt the Society and the Evangelical Synod sought to be a community that lived by the light, compassion, and teachings of Jesus, as well as by the work of Christ on the cross and the wonderment and grace of the resurrection. Did they do so to perfection? Obviously not. Yet these German-speaking immigrants of nearly two hundred years ago understood who they were. They perceived themselves more as a *Liebesgemeinschaft* (a community of love) than as a *Lehrgemeinschaft* (a community of doctrine). In establishing hospitals, orphanages, and other ministries of service to others, they insisted that it is "the love of Jesus that compels us." The text of *The Evangelical Catechism* seeks to reflect this foundational commitment.

Catechism as Instruction in the Basics

Throughout the history of the Christian Church, communion with Jesus has been foundational to the life of the community. In the early centuries, when the Church faced a struggle to live its faith in hostile surroundings, the Lord's Supper offered the abiding presence of Christ to those who where his followers. Nourished for the journey of faith at the communion table, young and old had first to be baptized. This crucial moment was usually preceded by a period of instruction. They were taught, among other things, to confess that "Jesus is Lord" in distinction to the other "lords" who sought their allegiance. As we know from the history of the Church, to be a Christian was, at certain times and places, a costly, dangerous thing. Taking one's place at the communion table could be risky, but it was also seen as preparatory to participation in the great banquet that would occur with the dawning of the kingdom of God. Women and men, rich and poor, the weak and the strong, the God-fearing and the self-centered were welcome, and, it was believed, all the angels in heaven rejoiced.

According to Scripture, at first there were no lines drawn around the table where Jesus was present. There were no tests and no formulas the baptized were required to recite. Table fellowship included all sorts and conditions of humanity. Tax collectors and sinners were welcome. Jesus reached out to the woman at the well. He beckoned Zacchaeus, hanging out on the limb of a tree. Such, Scripture proclaims, is the grace and generosity of the One who has come to bring us "new life."

In the early Church, baptism into the death and resurrection of Christ marked a "new birth." One was born from above by water and the Spirit. Baptism was understood not primarily as a human undertaking, but evidence of the radical commitment of the Creator of heaven and earth to the world and to the very least of those who dwell in it: people like ourselves. Those who sought to build their lives on the solid foundation of the grace of God were summoned to know who God is and the ways in which the heart of God beats for the whole creation. As the early hope of the immediate return of Christ began to fade, the Church faced the reality that his second coming would occur at some time in the future. But what to think and what to do in the meantime? Seeking to live "in Christ," they recalled the stories of Jesus. They remembered his crucifixion. They celebrated his resurrection, his ascension, and the sending of the Holy Spirit on the day of Pentecost. Teaching grew in importance.

The *First Apology* of Justin Martyr (second century C.E.), a text by one of the early Christian teachers, appeared around the year 148 C.E. This document reflects a belief that in baptism there occurs not only the forgiveness of sins, but entry into the "new life." Later testimony of the Church mothers and fathers shows that periods of preparation for the new life ranged from a few weeks to three months, three years, or even longer. A document known as the *Apostolic Tradition* of Hippolytus of Rome (believed to have died a martyr in the third century) refers to three years of teaching preceding baptism and first communion.[1]

There is a sentence in the writings of Tertullian (third century) that describes what was taking place as newly instructed individuals entered into the life of the Church: "But we, little fishes, after the example of Jesus Christ, are born in water, nor have we safety in any other way than by permanently abiding in water."[2] Many centuries later Luther echoed this idea, saying that there is a sense in which a Christian "lives in the water." The Christian life came to be understood as a daily immersion into the depths of Christ's sacrifice and a continuous participation in the healing power of the resurrection.

Throughout several centuries, Christians developed periods of instruction for those who desired baptism. A "catechumenate" (period of teaching) came to precede admission to holy communion. The "catechumens" were "hearers of the word," and their nurture in the biblical story and in the faith of the early Church was considered of vital importance. It was not uncommon for those new to the Christian faith to continue to hear the word for three years prior to their admission to the eucharist. Canon XIV of the First Council of Nicea (fourth century) required a period of three years of instruction for those who were to be baptized. Basic elements in teaching came to include the Apostles' Creed, the Ten Commandments, and the Lord's Prayer. During Lent, the great Cyril of Jerusalem (fourth century) presented a series of eighteen prebaptismal addresses to the candidates for baptism. These were related primarily to the Creed. During the weeks of Eastertide, five additional speeches on the "mysteries" of the faith were given by Cyril to the newly baptized. An arcane discipline emerged whereby the Creed and the Lord's Prayer were kept secret from the candidates until the moment of baptism arrived.[3] With Theodore of Mopsuestia (fourth century), the candidates for baptism appeared in sackcloth and were barefoot. The roughness of the cloth and the sores on their feet were intended as reminders of former sins. The linen stole that was placed over their heads signified the new freedom into which they emerged from the waters of the "new birth."[4]

The Heritage of the Reformation

Some years after the emperor Constantine established Christianity as the official church of the Roman Empire in the fourth century, the quality of teaching began to decline. By the time of the Protestant Reformation in the sixteenth century, the vitality of the catechumenate was a distant memory. Confirming the faith involved little or no instruction. It had become simply a matter of receiving a blessing by the laying on of hands. When Luther nailed his Ninety-five Theses to the door of the Castle Church in Wittenberg in 1517, the shaping of the new life of disciples of Jesus had been nearly lost in the Western Church. Luther described the teaching of the Church as little more than "monkey business." Godparents were still encouraged to teach their godchildren the Lord's Prayer, the Hail Mary, and the three Articles of the Apostles' Creed, but the quality of teaching had diminished severely. The Reformers sought to change this. An authentic baptismal theology re-emerged, reflecting the integrity and intensity of earlier teachers of the Church such as the great St. John Chrysostom and the revered St. Augustine in the fourth and fifth centuries.

For the Reformers, faith was understood as trust in what is proclaimed both in the Word of God and in baptism and the eucharist: grace to the fallen, our redemption in Christ, and eternal salvation. The young (and their parents!) needed to be nurtured in these realities. Luther's *Small Catechism* was published in 1529 with this in mind. It was crafted after a visit to congregations during which he was shocked by the lack of understanding of the faith of the Church among both the members of congregations *and* their clergy. The catechism was intended for the benefit of parents (and their pastors!) as they sought to instruct children in the foundations of faith. It is grace though faith that saves, the sixteenth-century Reformers proclaimed. But how shall this become known? It was a matter of the heart, to be sure, but it also included "belief of the mind" and "assent of the will."

The Protestant and Reformer at Strassburg, Martin Bucer, included in the baptism liturgy a public recitation of the Lord's Prayer and the Apostles' Creed, which godparents were also required to learn. His teaching of the young included the study of the Scriptures and knowledge of the Ten Commandments. Catechisms began to flourish at this time. Bucer introduced an examination of children that became a door through which the young were admitted to their first communion. First communion, which took place at various times in the Church Year — Christmas, Easter, and Pentecost — included the presentation of the confirmands, an examination of the contents of the catechism, prayers, and an invocation of the Holy Spirit intended to strengthen the young in the struggles of life ahead. The famous *Heidelberg Catechism,* created by Zacharias Ursinus (a student of Luther's colleague Philipp Melanchthon) and Caspar Olevianus, was widely used in places where the heritage of the Reformation took root. These innovations and their subsequent development have been part of the Lutheran, Reformed, and Anglican traditions in the Church to the present time, including the portion of the Church that became known in the nineteenth century as the Evangelical Synod of North America. The Reformation of the sixteenth century was rooted in faithful teaching, and it helped shape the Evangelical tradition and give it life.

In Essentials Unity,
In All Things Charity

What became the Evangelical Synod of North America in the 1870s — before merging in 1934 with the Reformed Church in the United States to form the Evangelical and Reformed Church — began in 1840 as a tiny, insignificant seed. Perhaps better said, it was a collection of little seeds scattered from Missouri and southern Illinois in the west, to northern Illinois, Wisconsin, and Michigan in the north, to Ohio, New York and elsewhere in the east. The congregations that eventually chose to join the Synod were founded primarily by German-speaking immigrants. They began arriving in the United States in the 1830s and 1840s. Some of the immigrants were educated in German universities; others had little formal education. Many were farmers and artisans, gifted with their hands. All were women and men and children who possessed the courage necessary to risk the long journey across the ocean to the uncertainties and enormous challenges that awaited them in the new world.

The roots of the faith of many of these immigrants went deep into the heart of the Evangelical Church of the Old Prussian Union, founded as a united Church in Germany in 1817, at the time of the three hundredth anniversary of the Protestant Reformation. The Prussian Union Church was composed of Lutheran and Reformed congregations that agreed to respect one another's theological differences and to live in the harmony of Christ. These congregations shared the heritage of the Reformation and teachers like Luther, Zwingli, Calvin, Melanchthon, Bucer, and Brenz. It is impossible to understand either *The Evangelical Catechism* or the Evangelical tradition apart from the influence of such teachers. But many of the congregations were shaped as well by another enormous force: the Pietist movements of the seventeenth and eighteenth centuries and the nineteenth-century ecumenical mission houses at Basel, Barmen, Bremen, and elsewhere. This was particularly true of the Evangelical Church Society of the West, a forerunner of the Evangelical Synod. Soon after its formation, the Society produced the catechism. Combining deep commitments to mission, to the unity of the Church, to an educated clergy, and to deeds of mercy that are the fruits of faith, the pietist spirit rests deep within what became well known, after several revisions, as *The Evangelical Catechism*.

The first ministers crafted a simple statement of the theology that would guide the Church Society of the West. Refined more than once, this statement reflects the spirit both of the Society and of what would eventually become the Evangelical Synod of North America.

> We recognize the Evangelical Church as that communion which acknowledges the Holy Scriptures of the Old and the New Testament as the Word of God and as the sole and infallible rule of faith and life, and accepts the interpretation of the Holy Scriptures as given in the symbolic books of the Lutheran and the Reformed Church, the most important being: the Augsburg Confession, Luther's and the Heidelberg Catechisms, in so far as they agree; but where they disagree, we adhere strictly to the passages of Holy Scripture bearing on the subject, and avail ourselves of the liberty of conscience prevailing in the Evangelical Church.[5]

The Evangelical Catechism appeared in 1847. It was the first major publication of the Church Society of the West. It was born in a time of crisis. Among the pastors, there was a determination that children baptized into the Christian faith should be nurtured in the teachings that had sustained the Church through the thick and thin of history. The authors faced stiff resistance, not from within the Society, but from beyond it. On the one side were the "rationalists," who despised even the idea of faith and attacked the Society mercilessly. On the other side were the "religious," who believed that a church that sought harmony between Lutheran and Reformed traditions was a false and despicable compromise, an unworthy assault on orthodox Protestant belief that did not properly value the Church's (Lutheran) theological heritage. (Echoes of these struggles of long ago have accompanied us into the twenty-first century, as "liberal" and "conservative" understandings of the faith of the Church reveal.)

The catechism of 1847 was intended to be neither Lutheran nor Reformed, but rather a combination of the most vital teachings of both traditions.[6] It was revised in the 1850s, primarily by Andreas Irion (1823–1870), a young, gifted theologian who served as a professor at the theological seminary founded in 1850 by the Evangelical Church Society of the West at Marthasville, Missouri. (The school later moved to St. Louis, where it became known as Eden Theological Seminary.) A native of Wurttemburg in southwestern Germany, where Lutheran influence was strong, Irion studied at the Basel Mission House for five years. There he was significantly influenced by the ecumenical spirit of pietism. He was about to be sent to Russia to serve as a pastor among German-speaking immigrants, but the plans changed and he emigrated to the United States instead. Irion began teaching at the seminary in 1853, six years after the original publication of the catechism. By 1856, he was urging an abbreviation of the catechism of 1847. He, along with others, completed that project in 1862. Carl Schneider, the leading historian of the Evangelical Church Society of the West, notes that the catechism of

1862 was criticized by some as being "too Lutheran." Other critics, with Lutheran leanings, considered it to be merely a "patchwork." There were those who called it neither Lutheran nor Reformed, but simply "Irion." This catechism was revised slightly in the 1890s, and a new edition appeared in 1929. It was a vital teaching tool in the life of the Evangelical Synod of North America well into the twentieth century.

The Evangelical Catechism as Helper, Nurturer, and Friend

The Evangelical Catechism is best understood as a guide, a helper, a nurturer, and a friend of those who confess the Christian faith. It is not a ruler — such as those used in the days of corporal punishment to rap the knuckles of inattentive students — poised and ready to keep the Church in line. Taking a nondogmatic approach, the catechism did not attempt to force the truth about God and ourselves down anyone's throat. Instead, it sought to assist the members of the Evangelical Synod, and especially the children, in taking those initial fragile, yet important, steps that are so crucial along the path of discipleship. It confessed there are some needful things that should be taken on the journey of faith, things that should be studied and learned by those who seek to live a new life, after the pattern of Jesus Christ.

The catechism offers a biblical foundation for what is taught in each section of the little book. It became for many the "confessional statement" of the entire Evangelical Synod of North America in the 1870s and beyond, pointing to Scripture as the ultimate guide to the life and witness of the Church. The text reflects both the generous faith of Basel/Wurttemburgian pietism, and many of the theological insights of the Reformation. It affirms what became the motto of the Evangelical

Synod of North America, namely, "In essentials unity, in nonessentials liberty, in all things charity."[7] As noted above, the Synod did not want the Church to be fighting over doctrine. While the Church's teaching is vital and should be studied prayerfully, wrestled with as necessary, and defended vigorously as required, even more crucial is the generous spirit of Christ who summons the Church to unity in the love of God and neighbor.[8]

The evangelicals wished to entrust to their children a deep, yet simple, faith that was thoughtful, biblically anchored, and theologically sound, as well as open, generous, compassionate, and true to the life and passion of Jesus. The catechism, however imperfect, is a testament to what has since become a cornerstone of the faith proclaimed within the life of the United Church of Christ: "There is yet more light and truth to break forth from God's holy Word." It sought to speak to its time. It challenges us to speak to ours.

Foundational to the catechism, however, is a belief that it is "God's holy Word," and not human speculation or theories, which provides the framework for the life, witness, and vocation of the Church. There is room for disagreement and different perspectives on matters relating to the biblical story, its truth, and the presence of Jesus in the compelling events of our time. But we all live from "One Lord, one faith, one baptism, one God and Father of us all, who is above all, and in all, and through all" (Eph. 4:5–6). The Scriptures and the Holy Spirit are to guide us, and the great texts of the Reformation and the early Church fathers and mothers remain a lens through which to view the issues at stake. The Evangelical tradition holds that this requires theological commitment, study, and prayer.

Throughout *The Evangelical Catechism*, the faith of the Church is presented not as a *possession* of the believer, but as a gift from beyond us; faith is evidence of the grace of God among very imperfect and undeserving, yet grateful people.

This is clearly seen in the response to Question 101, where the catechism borrows from Luther's summary of the Third Article of the Apostles' Creed: "I believe that I can not by my own reason or strength believe in my Lord Jesus Christ, or come to him; but the Holy Spirit has called me by the gospel, enlightened me with his gifts, sanctified and preserved me in the true faith." The catechism affirms that the *initiative* in faith remains with God, whose nature and goodness are revealed in Jesus Christ through the power of the Holy Spirit. The subjective temptation, sometimes found in pietism, to make the faith of the *Church* so deeply personal that it disappears as the faith of the Church and becomes "my faith" alone, is fairly well avoided here. It is not *we* who have to take care of God by *our* sturdy belief, but *God* who takes care of *us* by the wonder of divine love, reaching out to us in mercy and kindness (as wonderfully depicted in the famous painting by Michelangelo on the ceiling of the Sistine Chapel in Rome). And yet, the catechism remains true to the deeply personal nature of faith as well when, at the end, in response to the final question, "What does our communion daily require of us?" it breathlessly exclaims in words that remained dear to generations of those who were nurtured in the Christian faith as part of the Evangelical Synod:

> Lord Jesus, for thee I live, for thee I suffer, for thee I die!
> Lord Jesus, thine will I be in life and death!
> Grant me, O Lord, eternal salvation!
> Amen.[9]

Making the Faith Our Own

The Evangelical Catechism presents us with a challenge. The catechism is a statement of belief that guided the lives of those who knew something of both the burdens and the exhilaration of attempting to follow Jesus. We can be thankful that we have that statement as a resource for our faith. But the catechism also challenges us to take on the many new and intriguing issues that face us. The most critical of all may be how we permit the Christian faith to take root deeply and authentically within us in the times through which we are living, in a situation that is so different from that of our forebears. A common thread, though, remains clear and presents a perhaps even larger challenge: the catechism reminds us of our obligation not only to teach and read and continue learning, but also to sink to our knees in prayer. This is especially critical for us in the United Church of Christ, where we often find ourselves swimming in an ocean of activities and good deeds. It is not by coincidence that the hands of the martyred Oscar Romero, the "pastor of the poor" in El Salvador, were invariably seen to be folded in prayer. The catechism calls out, in a modest, yet authentic way, for thinking, reflecting, studying, and responding with courage and faith to a new set of circumstances. It urges us to try, where we can, to make the faith of our forebears our own. We cannot do that, however, by blithely or sloppily or offhandedly adopting tenets they took as *critical.* We have to figure this out. And the only place to do that is on our knees.

The catechism is a reminder that where God is truly God in the life of the Church, we are likely to be shaken to the foundation of our being by the sheer wonder of the biblical story and the fact that the Creator and Redeemer of the world and of every living thing has made us little less than Godself (Psalm 8). The catechism is a reminder that where God is truly God, those who seek to live by faith will often be found asking: "Who are we that you are mindful of us?" and that you take time for us, and that you come among us and dwell with us "full of grace and truth"?

We know, deep in our souls, that where this happens, the Word of God entrusted to us is not always going to be comfortable. "My thoughts are not your thoughts; neither are your ways my ways, says the Lord" (Isaiah 55). Is it not true that when it comes to the teaching of the Church, there are many joys, but also many demands, expectations, and obligations? Perhaps by reading through this old catechism again, you shall be reminded of this fact. That would be evidence of the grace to which *The Evangelical Catechism* seeks to point.

Sometimes we are tempted merely to nod in the direction of biblical claims and assurances. We can point to plenty of evidence around us that we allow ourselves to live at ease alongside the radical testimony of baptism and eucharist, often totally ignoring the summons to life embedded deeply within the signs and wonders of our faith. We smile when we ought to weep. We remain calm when we ought to tremble. We are silent when we ought to speak out. We shout when we ought to remain silent. We muse about holy things and debate them endlessly when we should be falling to our knees.

Should not the testimony of the Gospel of Jesus Christ, by its very nature, cause us to raise questions, deepen our thinking, lead us into places of doubt, and also to moments of miraculous wonder, awe, and passion for the faith we proclaim? Does not trusting God with our lives result in an appreciation of surprise and mystery? And does not faith, where it is authentic, not only lift us to great heights, but also bend us toward the depths of human existence? Faith carries us to places where there is nothing but wilderness and compels us toward the cross, into contemporary crucifixions that are the daily reality, if not of ourselves, then of countless numbers of our neighbors. Where the Christian faith is confessed are we not compelled to perceive the world from the pathos of the cross and thus from the depths where God is well-known, deep within the suffering of the world? The fact remains, as the catechism reminds us, that God becomes poor, God suffers and is stripped naked on the cross by the cruelty and avarice of the world. Yet God in Christ has overcome the world. The cross and resurrection of Jesus Christ remain the heart of the catechism and the center of the Evangelical heritage. In the Evangelical tradition, John Calvin's description of the Church as a series of resurrections from the dead makes sense.

The Evangelical Catechism points us, in its modest way, toward the realities of our lives, the joys and sorrows of human existence. It is a confession that faith — in the God who in Jesus kisses the earth and holds fallen humanity as close to the heart as a loving mother embraces her dear children — is a divine gift. It teaches that the obligations and responsibilities of faith are never meant to impede or suffocate the Church; they are meant, rather, to sustain and uphold our lives, preventing the hope that is in us from succumbing to habit, preventing love from being bartered and truth from being flattened, compromised, or emptied by the hollow substitutes for God we sometimes embrace. In the end, as at the beginning, the catechism calls us to accept with humility and joy our vocation as teachers and servants of the Word and to remain students and learners all our days.

We are continuously summoned to think, pray, explore, and risk. We are summoned to take with joyful and profound seriousness our vocation as servants of the Word and witnesses to the Gospel. God's radical commitment to the world in Jesus Christ is a fact to which we are called to respond by virtue of our baptism. *The Evangelical Catechism* presents us not so much with a nostalgic look backward, but with a challenge to embrace the faith entrusted to the communion of saints as we face the world today and tomorrow. Just as contemporary voices from diverse heritages bring gifts, challenges, and encouragement to the United Church of Christ, so this catechism raises its voice on behalf of the "new life" that is God's gift to us all in Christ.

The Evangelical tradition is not perfect. But it is honest. It is faithful. The catechism points with a bent finger, like John the Baptist, to the truth of *God among us* as that tradition, in a small and unique part of the Church and at a particular point in time, perceived it. The evangelicals who produced the catechism would be among the first to urge that we learn only what we *can* from them. They would encourage us to set the rest aside and to press on with the more vital and urgent task of bearing our own witness to the Gospel amid the storms that rage, the contradictions that confront us, the floods of injustice and violence that threaten to overcome the world, and the ravaging fires of indifference that burn in defiance of the biblical longing for peace and reconciliation in the world. We can say with certainty that we "do" catechesis differently today.[10] *The Evangelical Catechism* does not tell us precisely how to do this.[11] It invites us simply to press on with the task, for there are few things more vital to the integrity of the Church and to the life of the world. *The Evangelical Catechism* is best received as one would welcome a dear friend with whom we have occasional reunions even as our paths diverge and go in various directions.

The great innovator and pietist Philipp Jakob Spener remarked that each generation of believers stands upon the shoulders of those who have gone before it. Among those forebears there are some giants. We should not be ashamed, Spener suggested, to seek them out, to listen to them critically, carefully, and hopefully. We should not be ashamed to learn from them and give thanks that by standing on their strong, broad shoulders we are allowed to gain a better perspective on the faith we proclaim and the world in which we proclaim it. This is most certainly true!

Notes on the Translation

The translation is based on several editions of *The Evangelical Catechism* of 1929 as well as the earlier editions of 1892–1896 (when the catechism appeared both in German and in English) and the original revision of the catechism of 1847, dating from 1862. In this attempt to translate or restate *The Evangelical Catechism* for the twenty-first century, I have presented the various sections of the catechism in the order in which they appeared in 1929, when the last restatement was published. But I have made one exception: the Ten Commandments. I have included the Commandments here as Part I, as they originally appeared in the nineteenth-century editions of the catechism and as they continue to appear in Luther's *Small Catechism,* one of the three doctrinal statements that remained particularly important to the Evangelical Synod of North America. Thus, the catechism is presented in this order:

Introduction

Part I   The Ten Commandments

Part II   The Attributes of God

Part III The Three Articles of the Christian Faith

Part IV   Prayer

Part V   The Sacrament of Holy Baptism

Part VI   The Sacrament of the Lord's Prayer

A case can certainly be made that it is true to the Evangelical tradition to revise and rework the catechism in light of fresh, new, biblical, theological, and sociological insights within the Church and in the world around us. Were *The Evangelical Catechism* to be completely rewritten today, it would

surely present the faith in the context of the societal realities of our time. These realities are shaking the foundations
of life in the twenty-first century, including how the Christian
faith is to be understood and proclaimed in the face of natural
and human-initiated disasters, hunger, violence, homelessness,
poverty, warfare, and the enormity of human suffering that
contradicts the teaching of the Church almost everywhere we
look. All this would be viewed also, of course, through another
reality that remains crucial to this tradition: the incarnation,
the cross, and the resurrection of Jesus Christ, and the grace,
mercy, peace, benevolence and eternal hope without which
Christian tradition cannot be properly understood.

As it is, the sections of the catechism devoted to the Ten
Commandments, the Attributes of God, Prayer, Baptism, and
the Lord's Supper are properly understood only through the
lens of divine grace, as revealed in Jesus Christ. An attempt to
strike this note is made in the Introduction to the catechism.
The location of the Apostles' Creed (with its Three Articles)
at the center of the catechism, where the Evangelical tradition placed it, serves, I believe, a particular purpose. It helps
express the fact that the wonder of God's grace in Jesus Christ,
in the benevolent acts of creation, and in the loving gift of the
Holy Spirit, is at the heart of everything else in the catechism,
like the sun at the center of the solar system. It is God's grace
in Christ that gives light to everything else in this little book.
Thus, the Apostles' Creed does not appear first, or at the edge,
but in the middle, at the heart and center of the catechism.

One other note: True to my understanding of the Evangelical tradition, I have left most of the catechism intact, as it
appeared to previous generations, respecting what the mothers and fathers in this tradition sought to confess. But I have
also, in faithfulness to this tradition, in accord with its spirit,
and similarly to previous approaches taken over the past 150
years, made some adjustments. I have added several questions

and deleted a couple of others, while adjusting some of the biblical texts offered in support of the various questions and their responses. For example, in the 1929 edition, a question is asked about faith. I have added two additional questions, about hope and love, in accord with St. Paul's teaching in 1 Corinthians 13. In the translation that follows, I have also, while focusing on the reality of "divine grace," included questions about the realities of "costly grace" and "cheap grace," terms that became well-known to the Church after the 1929 edition of the catechism was published. In addition, the text of the Beatitudes is included in this translation as part of the body of the catechism itself, rather than as a preface (as in 1929). Readers may recognize several vital and familiar sentences, adopted from the famous Barmen Declaration of 1934, woven into the catechism in one or two places. Students of the Evangelical tradition will note that I have left the final question in the catechism, "What does our communion daily require of us?" and its profoundly eloquent and heartfelt response, just as they have been handed down and confessed from one generation to the next through all the years.

Notes to the Introduction

1. Among the great teachers of the early Church, Origen (Origenes Adamantius, c. 182–c. 251 C.E.) included in his instruction of those preparing for baptism, the story of Moses, Israel's miraculous crossing the Red Sea, the crossing of the Jordan River, and a baptismal theology anchored in Romans 6. In parts of the Church, teaching took place in Epiphany and highlighted the baptism of Jesus by John the Baptist at the Jordan. In other places, instruction took place during the forty days of Lent, culminating in the observance of Good Friday, baptism into Christ, and the celebration of the resurrection at Easter.

2. Quintus Septimius Florens Tertullian, "On Baptism," dating from around 200 C.E.

3. Dietrich Bonhoeffer advocated the recovery of the "arcane discipline" during the course of the "Church struggle" in Germany in the twentieth century, urging that the Evangelical Church affirm the basics of the Christian faith in hiddenness, while publicly giving expression to the faith solely by prayer and the deed.

4. For a thorough and exact account of this period see Maxwell E. Johnson, *The Rites of Christian Initiation: Their Evolution and Interpretation* (Collegeville, Minn.: Liturgical Press, 2007).

5. The words "Evangelical" and "evangelicals" have come to possess a variety of meanings in recent decades. The terms as used here reflect a joyous devotion to the good news of God's love and truth revealed in Jesus Christ. An "evangelical" in this sense is a bearer of good news, that is, the Gospel, a grateful ambassador or messenger who shares with others the wonder he or she has seen in the marvelous activity of God in Christ. It is in this sense that the Evangelical Synod of North America understood itself and its vocation.

6. Initial drafts of the catechism were composed and revised by a small committee of pastors of the Evangelical Church Society of the West. The leader of this group and a driving force behind the project appears to have been one of the founders of the Church Society, Louis E. Nollau (1810–1869), who came from Reichenbach/Oberlausitz, not far from the ancient city of Gorlitz in what today is eastern Germany. Trained at the Barmen Mission House, he was sent as a missionary to the Nez Percé Indians in the West, but for a variety of reasons he remained in Missouri, where he became active in serving the growing German-speaking population in and around St. Louis. Drafts of the catechism were finally approved after revisions made primarily by Adolph H. Baltzer (1817–1880). Baltzer had studied in Berlin and Halle under some of the most famous teachers of the Church in nineteenth-century Germany (Neander, Tholuck, and others). In 1845 he was sent by the Bremen Missionary Society to southern Illinois and he later became president of the Evangelical Synod of North America.

7. These words appear not only above the entrance to Eden Theological Seminary in Webster Groves, Missouri, but were also printed on the masthead of Philip Schaff's influential ecumenical

newspaper, *Der Deutsche Kirchenfreund,* published for the first time in 1848. Schaff remained a friend of the Evangelical Church Society of the West and its successors throughout his life. The famous words quoted here have been attributed to Rupertus Meldenius (pseudonym for Peter Meiderlin, 1582–1651). Meiderlin was a German Lutheran theologian who, during the Thirty Years War, urged the teachers of the Church to employ moderation and love in their theological disputes. This remained a vital note sounded over and over again in the "Evangelical tradition."

8. This, of course, is not an original theme. It is reflected earlier in the efforts of the great "mediating theologians," people like Philipp Melanchthon (1497–1560) and Martin Bucer (1491–1551), who valiantly sought to overcome differences between Lutheran and Reformed perspectives at the time of the Reformation. It also reflects an aversion to the rigid orthodoxies of the seventeenth century. It acknowledges the teaching of brave and often very lonely ecumenical theologians like Georg Calixtus (1586–1656), who sought to walk in the footsteps of the irenic Melanchthon. It is Calixtus who believed the major object of theology is not the search for pure doctrine, but the nurturing of the Christian life; a theme that members of the Evangelical Synod also asserted. It is in line as well with the pietists Philipp Jakob Spener (1635–1705) and August Hermann Francke (1663–1727), who worked toward faith that was neither rigid nor demeaning of neighbor; faith that promised an end to the bickering, hardness of heart, and estrangement that marked the life of the Church prior to and during the murderous Thirty Years War (1618–1648). Not insignificantly, the theological seminary of the Evangelical Synod of the Northwest, located just north of Chicago, was named Melanchthon Seminary. It subsequently moved to what today is the campus of Elmhurst College.

9. Professor Lowell Zuck of Eden Seminary has suggested that the origin of these famous words, so beloved in the Evangelical Synod of North America, may rest in Roman Catholic circles. The words, "Jesus, I live to you, Jesus, I die to you, Jesus, I am yours in life and in death" have been attributed to Alphonsus Liguori, who is believed to have composed them in Latin in 1761 as part of Catholic devotions during Lent. Alfonso Maria di Liguori (1696–1787) has

been called the most important Catholic moralist of the eighteenth century. Canonized by Gregory XVI in 1839, he was made a "doctor of the Church" in 1871 by Pius IX. Armin Haeussler suggested years ago that these words, attributed to Liguori, inspired the most famous hymn of the Reformed Church in the United States, "Jesus, I Live to Thee," believed by many to have been composed by Henry Harbaugh (1817–1867) around 1860.

10. Dietrich Bonhoeffer (1906–1945) created two catechisms that have survived. The first, in 1931, was called *By Faith Alone*. It included 40 questions and was composed in Berlin with his friend Franz Hildebrandt (1909–1985). The second, with nearly 170 questions, appeared in 1936 while Bonhoeffer was serving as dean of the underground resistance seminary of the "Confessing Church" at Finkenwalde, near the Baltic Sea. The early catechism did not include the Apostles' Creed in its traditional form or the Lord's Prayer. It embraced Martin Luther's Trinitarian statement of faith with its famous words: "But this is the Christian faith: to know what you should do and what has been given you." Bonhoeffer introduces subjects such as war, peace, and the unity of the Church, in ways not done before. In response to the question "Who is evangelical?" the 1931 catechism reads: One "who rejoices in the grace of God, confesses the name of Christ, and asks for the Holy Spirit." One "who is ready for the rule of God, is not afraid of the power of others, and is sure of the final end of all things." One "who hears God speaking through the preaching of the Word, who loves God's church and lives by God's forgiveness."

11. Contemporary pedagogy presents fresh challenges and opportunities for those who would teach Christian essentials. The use of film, poetry, historical and modern novels, short stories, television, the Internet, classical and modern art, music, and the ability to travel, open up wonderful possibilities for creative and passionate teaching. Exploring biblical stories in the Hebrew Bible and the profound meaning of the parables of Jesus in relation to modern experiences of tragedy, beauty, contradiction, hope, cruelty, wonder, benevolence, courage, sacrifice, emptiness, confusion, forgiveness, love, and other realities, opens wide the door of challenge and possibility to the imaginative teacher. Study of the UCC "Statement of Faith," the modern

"Kairos" document, the important "Barmen Declaration," and Martin Luther King's urgent "Letter from Birmingham Jail," among many other texts, offers magnificent opportunities for creative thought and conversation among children and the young as they seek to make connections between word and deed, what we profess and how we live the Christian faith. In a time when surveys show that, only 40 percent of Americans can name more than four of the Ten Commandments and 12 percent believe Joan of Arc to be Noah's wife (*Harper's Magazine,* August 2005), the challenge to recover the basics also remains profound.

THE EVANGELICAL
CATECHISM

Introduction

1. What should be our chief concern in life?

Our chief concern in life should be to seek after the kingdom of God and to hold fast to the righteousness of God in all its life-giving, life-sustaining, life-transforming power.

a. Matt. 6:33. "But strive first for the kingdom of God and his righteousness, and all these things will be given to you as well."

b. Mark 4:30–32. [Jesus] also said: "With what can we compare the kingdom of God, or what parable will we use for it? It is like a mustard seed, which, when sown upon the ground, is the smallest of all the seeds on earth, yet when it is sown it grows up and becomes the greatest of all shrubs, and puts forth large branches, so that the birds of the air can make nests in its shade."

c. Ps. 145:13. Your kingdom is an everlasting kingdom, and your dominion endures throughout all generations. The Lord is faithful in all his words, and gracious in all his deeds.

d. Matt. 5:6. "Blessed are those who hunger and thirst for righteousness, for they will be filled."

Cf. Mark 1:14–15; Mark 4:26–32; Luke 13:18–21.

2. How do we obtain this kingdom?

The kingdom of God is made known to us and the righteousness of God is revealed to us in the Gospel of Jesus Christ. "He is the one Word of God we are called to trust and obey in life and in death" (from the Barmen Declaration of 1934).

a. Ps. 16:11. You show me the path of life. In your presence there is fullness of joy.

b. John 1:1–4. In the beginning was the Word, and the Word was with God, and the Word was God. He was in the beginning with God. All things came into being through him, and without him not one thing came into being. What has come into being in him was life, and the life was the light of all people.

c. Ps. 25:4–5. Make me to know your ways, O Lord; teach me your paths. Lead me in your truth, and teach me, for you are the God of my salvation.

d. John 1:14. And the Word became flesh and lived among us, and we have seen his glory, the glory as of a father's only son, full of grace and truth.

Cf. Col. 1:15–20; John 6:51; Acts 16:31; Rom. 1:16–17.

3. In our seeking the kingdom of God, in our longing for God's righteousness, and in our hope of inheriting eternal life, what must we do?

We must place our trust and our hope in our Lord Jesus Christ, who is God's mighty claim upon our whole lives. Through him we are delivered from the idols of the world to free, joyous, and grateful service to the whole creation.

a. John 6:40. "This is indeed the will of my Father, that all who see the Son and believe in him may have eternal life; and I will raise them up on the last day."

b. Ps. 34:8. O taste and see that the Lord is good; happy are those who take refuge in him.

c. Ps. 96:1–5. O sing to the Lord a new song; sing to the Lord, all the earth. Sing to the Lord, bless his name; tell of his salvation from day to day. Declare his glory among the nations, his marvelous works among all the peoples. For great is the Lord, and greatly to be praised; he is to be revered above all gods. For all the gods of the peoples are idols, but the Lord made the heavens.

d. Rom. 5:1–2. Therefore, since we are justified by faith, we have peace with God through our Lord Jesus Christ, through whom we have obtained access to this grace in which we stand; and we boast in our hope of sharing the glory of God.

Cf. Ps. 71:17–18; Col. 1:9–14; Mark 8:27–33.

4. Where are we told about the promises of God, the joyous fact of our salvation, and God's astonishing love for the whole creation?

We are told about God's promises and the audaciousness of God's love for us all in the Holy Scriptures, which were written by people of faith who were moved by the Holy Spirit.

a. Ps. 119:105. Your word is a lamp to my feet and a light to my path.

b. Isa. 43:1. Do not fear, for I have redeemed you; I have called you by name, you are mine.

c. John 3:16. "For God so loved the world that he gave his only Son, so that everyone who believes in him may not perish but may have eternal life."

d. Ps. 25:4–5. Make me to know your ways, O Lord; teach me your paths. Lead me in your truth, and teach me, for you are the God of my salvation.

Cf. Ps. 33:1–5; Isa. 40:1–5; Isa. 53:1–9; Luke 2.

5. In what ways do the Scriptures reveal to us the purposes of God for our lives and for the life of the world around us?

God's purposes are made known to us in the Gospel of Jesus Christ and in the witness of the apostles, as well as in the Ten Commandments, in the prayers and songs of the psalmists, in the testimony of the biblical prophets, and in the faith and travail of the people of Israel.

a. John 13:13–15. "You call me Teacher and Lord — and you are right, for that is what I am. So if I, your Lord and Teacher, have washed your feet, you also ought to wash one another's feet. For I have set you an example, that you also should do as I have done to you."

b. Rom. 12:9–13. Let love be genuine; hate what is evil, hold fast to what is good; love one another with mutual affection; outdo one another in showing honor. Do not lag in zeal, be ardent in spirit, serve the Lord. Rejoice in hope, be patient in suffering, persevere in prayer. Contribute to the needs of the saints; extend hospitality to strangers.

c. Mark 12:30–31. "You shall love the Lord your God with all your heart, and with all your soul, and with all your mind, and with all your strength.... You shall love your neighbor as yourself. There is no other commandment greater than these."

d. Ps. 150:1–2. Praise the Lord! Praise God in his sanctuary; praise him in his mighty firmament! Praise him for his mighty deeds; praise him according to his surpassing greatness!

e. Mic. 6:8. He has told you, O mortal, what is good; and what does the Lord require of you but to do justice, and to love kindness, and to walk humbly with your God?

f. Deut. 6:4–7. Hear, O Israel: The Lord is our God, the Lord alone. You shall love the Lord your God with all your heart, and with all your soul, and with all your might. Keep these words that I am commanding you today in your heart. Recite them to your children and talk about them when you are at home and when you are away, when you lie down and when you rise.

Cf. 1 John 3:11–23; 1 Cor. 13; Deut. 5:1–21; Isa. 1:17; Exod. 14–15; Luke 5:1–11.

Part I

The Ten Commandments

6. Where is God's will for our lives presented to us in a concise form?

We find God's will for our lives concisely given to us in the Ten Commandments.

Cf. Exod. 20:1–17; Deut. 5:6–21.

7. What is the First Commandment?

"I am the Lord your God, who brought you out of the land of Egypt, out of the house of slavery; you shall have no other gods before me."

Cf. Exod. 20:2–3; Deut. 5:6–7.

8. What is meant by this Commandment?

God wants us to resist the temptation to commit idolatry, creating gods of our own, or serving them in any way. We are called, rather, to love, trust, fear, and obey God in all things.

a. 1 John 5:3. For the love of God is this, that we obey his commandments. And his commandments are not burdensome.

b. Ps. 37:5. Commit your way to the Lord; trust in him, and he will act.

c. Prov. 3:5–6. Trust in the Lord with all your heart, and do not rely on your own insight. In all your ways acknowledge him, and he will make straight your paths.

d. 1 Chron. 16:11–12. Seek the Lord and his strength, seek his presence continually. Remember the wonderful works he has done, his miracles, and the judgments he uttered.

Cf. Matt. 4:1–11.

9. What is the Second Commandment?

"You shall not make for yourself an idol, whether in the form of anything that is in heaven above, or that is on the earth beneath, or that is in the water under the earth. You shall not bow down to them or worship them."

Cf. Exod. 20:4–6; Deut. 5:8–10.

10. What is meant by this Commandment?

God wants us to resist the temptation to place our faith and our hope in any of the many gods that seek our allegiance, such as money, power, self-indulgence, pride, or the false gods of precious or lethal metal, or in violence and empire that abound in the world.

a. Isa. 42:6–8. "I am the Lord, I have called you in righteousness, I have taken you by the hand and kept you; I have given you as a covenant to the people, a light to the nations, to open the eyes that are blind, to bring out the prisoners from the dungeon, from the prison those who sit in darkness. I am the Lord, that is my name; my glory I give to no other, nor my praise to idols."

b. John 4:24. "God is spirit, and those who worship him must worship in spirit and truth."

Cf. Isa. 40:17–31; Ps. 100.

11. What is the Third Commandment?

"You shall not make wrongful use of the name of the Lord your God, for the Lord will not acquit anyone who misuses his name."

Cf. Exod. 20:7; Deut. 5:11.

12. What is meant by this Commandment?

God wants us to resist the temptation to misuse God's name for our own selfish purposes, for example, cheating or deceiving others in order to gain advantage over them, lying to others with pious, angry, or flowery words, or being part of any effort to beat the drums of violence and war in God's name.

a. Prov. 14:5. A faithful witness does not lie, but a false witness breathes out lies.

b. Ps. 57:1, 4–5. Be merciful to me, O God, be merciful to me, for in you my soul takes refuge; . . . until the destroying storms pass by. . . . I lie down among lions that greedily devour human prey; their teeth are spears and arrows, their tongues sharp swords. Be exalted, O God, above the heavens. Let your glory be over all the earth.

c. Ps. 50:15. "Call upon me in the day of trouble; I will deliver you, and you shall glorify me."

Cf. Luke 18:35–43; Ps. 92:1–2; Lev. 19:12.

13. What is the Fourth Commandment?

"Remember the sabbath day, and keep it holy."

Cf. Exod. 20:8–11; Deut. 5:12–15.

14. What is meant by this Commandment?

God wants us to resist the temptation to exhaust ourselves in work or to allow our souls to become hollow and empty by turning our backs on God's grace and truth. For Christians this means joyfully receiving the Gospel, gathering in community to hear God's Word, celebrating the sacraments of the Church, engaging in prayer and honoring the divine commitment to the world through lives of discipleship.

a. Ezek. 20:20. "Hallow my sabbaths that they may be a sign between me and you, so that you may know that I the Lord am your God."

b. Ps. 26:8, 12. O Lord, I love the house in which you dwell, and the place where your glory abides.... My foot stands on level ground; in the great congregation I will bless the Lord.

c. Col. 3:16–17. Let the word of Christ dwell in you richly; teach and admonish one another in all wisdom; and with gratitude in your hearts sing psalms, hymns, and spiritual songs to God. And whatever you do, in word or deed, do everything in the name of the Lord Jesus, giving thanks to God the Father through him.

d. Luke 11:28. "Blessed... are those who hear the word of God and obey it!"

Cf. Ps. 66:1–4; Ps. 95:1–7; Ps. 27.

15. What is the Fifth Commandment?

"Honor your father and your mother."

Cf. Exod. 20:12; Deut. 5:16.

16. What is meant by this Commandment?

God's will is that we honor our parents and that in the midst of life's joys, hopes, needs, and contradictions, we seek to be loyal to them, and that we also respect those who, by the will of God, govern justly over us.

a. Prov. 1:8. Hear, my child, your father's instruction, and do not reject your mother's teaching.

b. Eph. 6:1–3. Children, obey your parents in the Lord, for this is right. "Honor your father and mother" — this is the first commandment with a promise: "so that it may be well with you and you may live long on the earth."

c. Rom. 13:1. Let every person be subject to the governing authorities; for there is no authority except from God, and those authorities that exist have been instituted by God.

d. Acts 5:29. "We must obey God rather than any human authority."

Cf. Matt. 10:32–39.

17. What is the Sixth Commandment?

"You shall not murder."

Cf. Exod. 20:13; Deut. 5:17.

18. What is meant by this Commandment?

God's will is that we not kill anyone and that we not threaten, endanger, or embitter our own lives or the lives of our neighbors in any way. Rather, God expects that we assist our neighbors in their need and that, rather than injuring them, we seek their well-being in this life, in the joyful expectation of the life to come.

a. Eph. 4:32. Be kind to one another, tenderhearted, forgiving one another, as God in Christ has forgiven you.

b. Isa. 1:17. Learn to do good; seek justice, rescue the oppressed, defend the orphan, plead for the widow.

c. Matt. 5:43–45. "You have heard that it was said, 'You shall love your neighbor and hate your enemy.' But I say to you, Love your enemies and pray for those who persecute you, so that you may be children of your Father in heaven; for he makes his sun rise on the evil and on the good, and sends rain on the righteous and on the unrighteous."

d. Matt. 26:52. "Put your sword back into its place; for all who take the sword will perish by the sword."

Cf. Isa. 11:1–9; Mic. 4:1–4; Matt. 5:1–26; Prov. 24:1–3.

19. What is the Seventh Commandment?

"You shall not commit adultery."

Cf. Exod. 20:14; Deut 5:18.

20. What is meant by this Commandment?

God's will is that we not commit adultery, and that we resist all thoughts, words, and deeds that are faithless.

a. Matt. 5:8. "Blessed are the pure in heart, for they will see God."

b. Prov. 4:23. Keep your heart with all vigilance, for from it flow the springs of life.

c. 1 Cor. 6:19–20. Do you not know that your body is a temple of the Holy Spirit within you, which you have from God, and that you are not your own? For you were bought with a price; therefore glorify God in your body.

d. Ps. 19:14. Let the words of my mouth and the meditation of my heart be acceptable to you, O Lord, my rock and my redeemer.

Cf. Eph. 5:1–2.

21. What is the Eighth Commandment?

"You shall not steal."

Cf. Exod. 20:15; Deut. 5:19.

22. What is meant by this Commandment?

God's will is that we not steal from anyone and that we not rob or engage in theft, trickery, fraud, or any other unfair or dishonest dealings with anyone; rather that we seek to improve and protect our neighbor's possessions and livelihood.

a. Jer. 22:13. Woe to him who builds his house by unrighteousness, and his upper rooms by injustice; who makes his neighbors work for nothing, and does not give them their wages.

b. Deut. 25:13–15. You shall not have in your bag two kinds of weights, large and small. You shall not have in your house two kinds of measures, large and small. You shall have only a full and honest weight; you shall have only a full and honest measure.

c. Eph. 4:28. Thieves must give up stealing; rather let them labor and work honestly with their own hands, so as to have something to share with the needy.

d. Hab. 2:9, 10, 11. Alas for you who get evil gain for your houses, setting your nest on high.... You have devised shame for your house by cutting off many peoples;... The very stones will cry out from the wall, and the plaster will respond from the woodwork.

Cf. Prov. 3:27–31; Rom. 13:8–10.

23. What is the Ninth Commandment?

"You shall not bear false witness against your neighbor."

Cf. Exod. 20:16; Deut. 5:20.

24. What is meant by this Commandment?

God's will is that we do not tell lies about our neighbors, or slander or demean them in any way. God requires instead that we be truthful and sincere, protecting the honor, good name, and reputation of our neighbors.

a. Ps. 34:13–14. Keep your tongue from evil, and your lips from speaking deceit. Depart from evil, and do good; seek peace, and pursue it.

b. Eph. 4:25. So then, putting away falsehood, let all of us speak the truth to our neighbors, for we are members of one another.

c. Luke 6:37–38. "Do not judge, and you will not be judged; do not condemn, and you will not be condemned. Forgive, and you will be forgiven; give, and it will be given to you. A good measure, pressed down, shaken together, running over, will be put into your lap; for the measure you give will be the measure you get back."

d. Phil. 4:8–9. Finally, beloved, whatever is true, whatever is honorable, whatever is just, whatever is pure, whatever is pleasing, whatever is commendable, if there is any excellence and if there is anything worthy of praise, think about these things . . . and the God of peace will be with you.

Cf. Isa. 5:20–24; Matt. 5:43–48.

25. What is the Tenth Commandment?

"You shall not covet."

Cf. Exod. 20:17; Deut. 5:21.

26. What is meant by this Commandment?

God's will is that we do not become jealous of anything that is rightfully our neighbor's; instead that we find our deepest joy and the meaning and direction of our lives in God's loving care for us.

a. Ps. 37:3–4. Trust in the Lord, and do good; ... Take delight in the Lord, and he will give you the desires of your heart.

b. Prov. 23:26. My child, give me your heart, and let your eyes observe my ways.

c. Rom. 6:12. Therefore, do not let sin exercise dominion in your mortal bodies, to make you obey their passions.

d. Matt. 7:12. "In everything do to others as you would have them do to you; for this is the law and the prophets."

Cf. Luke 16:10–13.

27. How would you summarize the Ten Commandments?

We summarize the Ten Commandments with the words of Jesus, who teaches those who seek to follow him: " 'You shall love the Lord your God with all your heart, and with all your soul, and with all your mind.' This is the greatest and first commandment. And a second is like it: 'You shall love your neighbor as yourself.' On these two commandments hang all the law and the prophets."

Cf. Matt. 22:34–40.

28. What does God declare concerning these Commandments?

God declares: You shall keep my statutes and my ordinances; by doing so you shall live.

a. Lev. 18:4–5. My ordinances you shall observe and my statutes you shall keep, following them: I am the Lord your God. You shall keep my statutes and my ordinances; by doing so one shall live: I am the Lord.

b. Luke 10:25–28. Just then a lawyer stood up to test Jesus. "Teacher," he said, "what must I do to inherit eternal life?" He said to him, "What is written in the law? What do you read there?" He answered, "You shall love the Lord your God with all your heart, and with all your soul, and with all your strength, and with all your mind; and your neighbor as yourself." And he said to him, "You have given the right answer; do this, and you will live."

Cf. Matt. 7:24–27; Luke 6:46–49.

29. What does God mean by this declaration?

By this declaration God means that we trust the Commandments and seek to live in accord with them. The Commandments are not given to us in order to put us down or to keep us from enjoying our lives, but rather to guide us and to help us make our way through life with faith, a sense of purpose, meaning, and joy. The Commandments offer us the freedom to live out the purposes of our creation.

a. Prov. 16:16. How much better to get wisdom than gold! To get understanding is to be chosen rather than silver.

b. Ps. 119:144. Your decrees are righteous forever; give me understanding that I may live.

c. Ps. 1:1, 2, 3. Happy are those ... [whose] delight is in the law of the Lord.... They are like trees planted by streams of water, which yield their fruit in its season, and their leaves do not wither.

Cf. Luke 6:43–45.

30. Have you, or has anyone, ever perfectly kept the Commandments?

None of us has ever perfectly kept the Commandments of God. By nature, we are inclined to go our own way, forging our own path through life. Often, we live at a great distance from the will of God. Thus, we have little claim on God's grace and blessing.

a. Ps. 130:3–4. If you, O Lord, should mark iniquities, Lord, who could stand? But there is forgiveness with you, so that you may be revered.

b. Ps. 143:1–2. Hear my prayer, O Lord; give ear to my supplications in your faithfulness; answer me in your righteousness. Do not enter into judgment with your servant, for no one living is righteous before you.

c. Isa. 40:8. The grass withers, the flower fades; but the word of our God will stand forever.

Cf. Matt. 7:15–23; Luke 13:22–30.

31. Is there any way we can avoid alienation from God because of our inability to keep the Commandments?

Gracefully, God provides for us a way. We live by the mercy of God and our lives are redeemed by the love of God in Jesus Christ, in whom God's will for us has taken human form.

a. Ps. 6:4. Turn, O Lord, save my life; deliver me for the sake of your steadfast love.

b. Ps. 25:14–15. The friendship of the Lord is for those who fear him, and he makes his covenant known to them. My eyes are ever toward the Lord, for he will pluck my feet out of the net.

c. Ps. 30:11–12. You have turned my mourning into dancing; you have taken off my sackcloth and clothed me with joy, so that my soul may praise you and not be silent. O Lord my God, I will give thanks to you forever.

d. Ps. 135:3. Praise the Lord, for the Lord is good; sing to his name, for he is gracious.

Cf. Matt. 8:1–3; Matt. 8:14–17.

32. What has God by grace and mercy done to make this possible?

In the Gospel, we hear these words about Jesus: "For God so loved the world that he gave his only Son, so that everyone who believes in him may not perish but have eternal life." St. Paul puts it this way: "But when the fullness of time had come, God sent his Son, born of a woman, born under the law, in order to redeem those who were under the law, so that we might receive adoption as children." (John 3:16; Gal. 4:4–5)

Cf. Ps. 42:1–5; Luke 2:1–20.

Part II

The Attributes
of God

33. What is revealed about God's nature in the Bible?

The Bible reveals that there is One God and that God is Spirit, that God is Life, and that God is both Light and Love. In saying this we know that the words we use to describe God are incomplete and can only hint at the fullness of God. This is why we take to heart what God is saying to us in the birth, life, death, resurrection, and ascension of Jesus Christ.

a. Deut. 6:4. Hear, O Israel: The Lord is our God, the Lord alone.

b. John 4:24. "God is spirit, and those who worship him must worship in spirit and truth."

c. 1 John 5:20. And we know that the Son of God has come and has given us understanding so that we may know him who is true; and we are in him who is true, in his Son Jesus Christ. He is the true God and eternal life.

d. 1 John 1:5. This is the message we have heard from him and proclaim to you, that God is light and in him there is no darkness at all.

e. 1 John 4:7–8. Beloved, let us love one another, because love is from God; everyone who loves is born of God and knows God. Whoever does not love does not know God, for God is love.

Cf. Mark 10:46–52.

34. What is meant when it is said that "God is Life"?

"God is Life" means that God is eternal, that God's nature is steadfastly reliable and faithful, and that God is always present with us.

God is eternal:

a. Ps. 90:1–2. Lord, you have been our dwelling place in all generations. Before the mountains were brought forth, or ever you had formed the earth and the world, from everlasting to everlasting you are God.

b. Rev. 1:8. "I am the Alpha and the Omega," says the Lord God, who is and who was and who is to come, the Almighty.

c. Isa. 26:4. Trust in the Lord forever, for in the Lord God you have an everlasting rock.

Cf. John 1:1–5.

God's nature is steadfastly reliable and faithful:

a. Isa. 41:10. Do not fear, for I am with you, do not be afraid, for I am your God; I will strengthen you, I will help you, I will uphold you with my victorious right hand.

b. Ps. 111:1, 7–8. I will give thanks to the Lord with my whole heart. . . . The works of his hands are faithful and

just; all his precepts are trustworthy. They are established
forever and ever, to be performed with faithfulness and
uprightness.

Cf. Matt. 8:23–27; Luke 8:22–25.

God is always present with us:

a. Ps. 23:4. Even though I walk through the darkest valley,
I fear no evil; for you are with me; your rod and your
staff — they comfort me.

b. Acts 17:27–28. Indeed he is not far from each one of us.
For "In him we live and move and have our being."

c. Jer. 23:23–24. Am I a God near by, says the Lord, and
not a God far off? Who can hide in secret places so that I
cannot see them? says the Lord. Do I not fill heaven and
earth? says the Lord.

Cf. Ps. 139:7–18.

35. What is meant when it is said that "God is Light"?

"God is Light" means that God is faithful and true; it means
that God is all-knowing, all-wise, holy, almighty, and just.

God is faithful and true:

a. Ps. 119:89–90. The Lord exists forever; your word is
firmly fixed in heaven. Your faithfulness endures to
all generations; you have established the earth, and it
stands fast.

b. Deut. 32:1–4. Give ear, O heavens, and I will speak; let
the earth hear the words of my mouth. May my teaching
drop like the rain, and my speech condense like the dew;
like gentle rain on grass, like showers on new growth. For
I will proclaim the name of the Lord; ascribe greatness
to our God! The Rock, his work is perfect, and all his

ways are just. A faithful God, without deceit, just and upright is he.

Cf. Luke 18:35–42.

God is all-knowing:

a. Ps. 139:1–6. O Lord, you have searched me and known me. You know when I sit down and when I rise up; you discern my thoughts from far away. You search out my path and my lying down, and are acquainted with all my ways. Even before a word is on my tongue, O Lord, you know it completely. You hem me in, behind and before, and lay your hand upon me. Such knowledge is too wonderful for me; it is so high that I cannot attain it.

b. 1 Sam. 16:7. The Lord does not see as mortals see; they look on the outward appearance, but the Lord looks on the heart.

c. Matt. 6:8. "Your Father knows what you need before you ask him."

Cf. Matt. 7:7–11; Luke 11: 9–13.

God is all-wise:

a. Isa. 55:8–9. For my thoughts are not your thoughts, nor are your ways my ways, says the Lord. For as the heavens are higher than the earth, so are my ways higher than your ways and my thoughts than your thoughts.

b. Ps. 104:24–25, 27. O Lord, how manifold are your works! In wisdom you have made them all; the earth is full of your creatures. Yonder is the sea, great and wide, creeping things innumerable are there, living things both small and great.... These all look to you to give them their food in due season.

Cf. Mark 6:30–44; Mark 8:1–9.

God is holy:

a. Isa. 6:3. "Holy, holy, holy is the Lord of hosts; the whole earth is full of his glory."

b. Lev. 19:2. You shall be holy, for I the Lord your God am holy.

c. Rev. 15:3–4. Great and amazing are your deeds, Lord God the Almighty! Just and true are your ways, King of the nations! Lord, who will not fear and glorify your name? For you alone are holy. All nations will come and worship before you, for your judgments have been revealed.

d. 1 Pet. 1:15–16. As he who called you is holy, be holy yourselves in all your conduct; for it is written, "You shall be holy, for I am holy."

Cf. John 7:14–18.

God is almighty:

a. Ps. 33:8–9. Let all the earth fear the Lord; let all the inhabitants of the world stand in awe of him. For he spoke, and it came to be; he commanded, and it stood firm.

b. Job 33:4. The spirit of God has made me, and the breath of the Almighty gives me life.

c. Luke 1:37. For nothing will be impossible with God.

Cf. Exodus 14.

God is just:

a. Ps. 111:1–2, 7–8. I will give thanks to the Lord with my whole heart, in the company of the upright, in the congregation. Great are the works of the Lord, studied by all who delight in them.... The works of his hands are faithful and just; all his precepts are trustworthy. They are established forever and ever, to be performed with faithfulness and uprightness.

b. Ps. 145:17. The Lord is just in all his ways, and kind in all his doings.

c. Ps. 103:6. The Lord works vindication and justice for all who are oppressed.

Cf. Luke 18:1–8.

36. What is meant when it is said that "God is Love"?

"God is Love" means that God is merciful and gracious, that God is blessed and good.

God is merciful and gracious:

a. Ps. 103:8–11. The Lord is merciful and gracious, slow to anger and abounding in steadfast love. He will not always accuse; nor will he keep his anger forever. He does not deal with us according to our sins, nor repay us according to our iniquities. For as the heavens are high above the earth, so great is his steadfast love toward those who fear him.

b. Ps. 103:13. As a father has compassion for his children, so the Lord has compassion for those who fear him.

c. Ps. 103:17–18. The steadfast love of the Lord is from everlasting to everlasting on those who fear him, and his righteousness to children's children, to those who keep his covenant and remember to do his commandments.

d. Luke 6:36. "Be merciful, just as your Father is merciful."

Cf. Luke 8:40–55.

God is blessed:

a. Ps. 28:6–7. Blessed be the Lord, for he has heard the sound of my pleadings. The Lord is my strength and my shield; in him my heart trusts; so I am helped, and my heart exults, and with my song I give thanks to him.

b. 1 Pet. 1:3–4. Blessed be the God and Father of our Lord Jesus Christ! By his great mercy he has given us a new birth into a living hope through the resurrection of Jesus Christ from the dead, and into an inheritance that is imperishable, undefiled, and unfading.

Cf. John 8:1–11.

God is good:

a. Ps. 107:1–3. O give thanks to the Lord, for he is good; for his steadfast love endures forever. Let the redeemed of the Lord say so, those he redeemed from trouble and gathered in from the lands, from the east and from the west, from the north and from the south.

b. Ps. 36:5–6. Your steadfast love, O Lord, extends to the heavens, your faithfulness to the clouds. Your righteousness is like the mighty mountains, your judgments are like the great deep; you save humans and animals alike, O Lord.

c. Ps. 145:8–9. The Lord is gracious and merciful, slow to anger and abounding in steadfast love. The Lord is good to all, and his compassion is over all that he has made.

Cf. Mark 6:53–56.

37. What mystery about God is revealed in the Bible?

The Bible reveals to us the mystery that in the One God there are three persons; the Father, the Son, and the Holy Spirit, and that these three are one.

a. Eph. 2:13, 17–19. But now in Christ Jesus you who were far off have been brought near by the blood of Christ. . . . So he came and proclaimed peace to you who were far off and peace to those who were near; for through him both of us have access in one Spirit to the Father. So then you are no longer strangers and aliens, but you are citizens with the saints and also members of the household of God.

b. John 14:15–16. "If you love me, you will keep my commandments. And I will ask the Father, and he will give you another Advocate, to be with you forever."

c. Matt. 28:18–20. "All authority in heaven and on earth has been given to me. Go therefore and make disciples of all nations, baptizing them in the name of the Father and of the Son and of the Holy Spirit, and teaching them to obey everything that I have commanded you. And remember, I am with you always, to the end of the age."

Cf. Eph. 1:3–14; Matt. 3:16–17.

Part III

The Three Articles of the Christian Faith

38. In what creed does the Christian Church confess its faith in the Triune God?

The Christian Church confesses its faith in the Triune God in the Apostles' Creed.

The Apostles' Creed

I believe in God the Father almighty, Maker of heaven and earth.

I believe in Jesus Christ, his only Son, our Lord, who was conceived by the Holy Spirit, born of the Virgin Mary, suffered under Pontius Pilate, was crucified, died, and was buried; he descended into hell. On the third day he rose again; he ascended into heaven and is seated at the right hand of God, the Father almighty, from where he will come to judge the living and the dead.

I believe in the Holy Spirit, the one holy universal Christian Church, the communion of saints, the forgiveness of sins, the resurrection of the body, and the life everlasting. Amen.

THE FIRST ARTICLE
OF THE CHRISTIAN FAITH

39. What is the First Article of the Christian Faith?

I believe in God the Father almighty, Maker of heaven and earth.

40. What does the First Article of the Christian Faith confess?

The First Article confesses faith in God the Father and the work of creation.

a. Gen. 1:1–2. In the beginning when God created the heavens and the earth, the earth was a formless void and darkness covered the face of the deep.

b. Ps. 33:6–7. By the word of the Lord the heavens were made, and all their host by the breath of his mouth. He gathered the waters of the sea as in a bottle; he put the deeps in storehouses.

c. Heb. 11:3. By faith we understand that the worlds were prepared by the word of God, so that what is seen was made from things that are not visible.

Cf. Gen. 1 and 2; Ps. 148.

41. What do we mean when we confess faith in God the Father almighty, Maker of heaven and earth?

We confess that the Maker of heaven and earth is not a creation of human imagination or of desperate longing, but rather is truly God, who in mercy and compassion beyond our imagining has shaped the heavens and the earth.

a. Ps. 150:1–2, 6. Praise the Lord! Praise God in his sanctuary; praise him in his mighty firmament! Praise him for his mighty deeds; praise him according to his surpassing greatness! . . . Let everything that breathes praise the Lord!

b. Isa. 45:12. I made the earth, and created humankind upon it; it was my hands that stretched out the heavens, and I commanded all their host.

c. Isa. 64:4. From ages past no one has heard, no ear has perceived, no eye has seen any God besides you.

Cf. Ps. 8.

42. How does God constantly prove to be the Creator?

God constantly proves to be the Creator through a gracious and loving providence by which God preserves and governs all things.

a. Ps. 33:4–5. The word of the Lord is upright, and all his work is done in faithfulness. He loves righteousness and justice; the earth is full of the steadfast love of the Lord.

b. Ps. 40:11. Do not, O Lord, withhold your mercy from me; let your steadfast love and your faithfulness keep me safe forever.

Cf. John 11:1–44; Gen. 8:22.

43. What has God done for you?

I believe that God has called me and all creatures into being; that he has given me and still preserves my body and soul, eyes, ears, and all my members, my reason and all my senses, also food and clothing, home and family, and all my possessions.

44. What does God still do for you?

God daily and abundantly provides me with all the necessities of life, protects and preserves me from all danger.

45. Why does God do this for you?

God does all this through no merit or worthiness of mine, but solely out of divine goodness and mercy.

46. What do you owe God for all this?

For all this I owe God thanks, praise, faithfulness, service, and obedience in all things.

47. What are the angels?

The angels are evidence of God's grace and loving care for us. They are sent forth by God to do God's will and to serve God's purposes

a. Ps. 103:20–21. Bless the Lord, O you his angels, you mighty ones who do his bidding, obedient to his spoken word. Bless the Lord, all his hosts, his ministers that do his will.

b. Ps. 91:11–12. For he will command his angels concerning you to guard you in all your ways. On their hands they will bear you up, so that you will not dash your foot against a stone.

c. Ps. 34:7–8. The angel of the Lord encamps around those who fear him, and delivers them. O taste and see that the Lord is good; happy are those who take refuge in him.

Cf. Matt. 4:1–11.

48. Who are the principal creatures on earth?

The principal creatures on earth are human beings, created in the image of God so that we could know God and live in joyful, grateful fellowship with God.

a. Gen. 1:27. So God created humankind in his image, in the image of God he created them; male and female he created them.

b. Eph. 2:10. For we are what he has made us, created in Christ Jesus for good works, which God prepared beforehand to be our way of life.

Cf. Luke 10:38–42.

49. Have we lived as we were created?

No, we have not. Like those who have lived before us, we turn from the ways of God, living at a distance from God, allowing ourselves to be tempted by the power of evil. Our sin fractures our relationship with God. Turning our backs on God, we are emptied of truth. The result is stiff-necked, arrogant behavior, idolatry and other forms of faithlessness.

a. Isa. 55:8–9. For my thoughts are not your thoughts, nor are your ways my ways, says the Lord. For as the heavens are higher than the earth, so are my ways higher than your ways and my thoughts than your thoughts.

b. Matt. 23:24–25. "You blind guides! You strain out a gnat but swallow a camel!... you clean the outside of the cup and of the plate, but inside they are full of greed and self-indulgence."

c. 1 John 1:8. If we say that we have no sin, we deceive ourselves and the truth is not in us.

d. Luke 15:7. "I tell you, there will be more joy in heaven over one sinner who repents than over ninety-nine righteous persons who need no repentance."

e. Prov. 3:6. In all your ways acknowledge him, and he will make straight your paths.

Cf. Gen. 3; Luke 18:9–14; Luke 15:3–10.

50. What are the sad consequences of our turning from God's ways?

By our lack of faith and truthfulness and by the arrogance that sometimes consumes us, the strength and beauty of our creation in God's image have been compromised. We are tempted to live at a distance not only from God but also from our neighbors; as strangers to the whole creation. It is a deep and often painful alienation and a reality every generation experiences.

a. Luke 15:18–19. Father, I have sinned against heaven and before you; I am no longer worthy to be called your son; treat me as one of your hired hands.

b. Ps. 57:1. Be merciful to me, O God, be merciful to me, for in you my soul takes refuge; in the shadow of your wings I will take refuge, until the destroying storms pass by.

Cf. Luke 10:29–37.

51. Where do we stand as a result of this estrangement from God, our neighbors, and the whole creation?

We live alienated from the "new life" which is God's gift to us. This can bring heartbreak to us and misery to the world.

a. Ps. 119:28. My soul melts away for sorrow; strengthen me according to your word.

b. Ps. 107:19–20. They cried out to the Lord in their trouble, and he saved them from their distress; he sent out his word and healed them, and delivered them from destruction.

c. Isa. 35:10. The ransomed of the Lord shall return, and come to Zion with singing; everlasting joy shall be on their heads; they shall obtain joy and gladness, and sorrow and sighing shall flee away.

Cf. Matt. 19:16–22.

52. What is grace?

Grace is the wondrous, unmerited kindness of God toward us and the whole creation. God does not allow our heartbreak to endure or the misery of sin to have the last word. Instead, God takes the world by surprise, drawing near to us in infinite mercy, embracing sinful humanity and the very least among us with unbounded love and astonishing humility.

a. Isa. 40:28–31. Have you not known? Have you not heard? The Lord is the everlasting God, the Creator of the ends of the earth. He does not faint or grow weary; his understanding is unsearchable. He gives power to the faint, and strengthens the powerless. Even youths will faint and be weary,... but those who wait for the Lord shall renew their strength, they shall mount up with wings like eagles, they shall run and not be weary, they shall walk and not faint.

b. John 1:17. The law indeed was given through Moses; grace and truth came through Jesus Christ.

c. Rom. 3:23–24. Since all have sinned and fall short of the glory of God; they are now justified by his grace as a gift, through the redemption that is in Christ Jesus.

d. Eph. 1:4–6. He chose us in Christ before the foundation of the world to be holy and blameless before him in love. He destined us for adoption as his children through Jesus Christ, according to the good pleasure of his will, to the praise of his glorious grace that he freely bestowed on us in the Beloved.

Cf. Luke 15:11–32; Hosea 14:1–7; Mark 5:1–20.

53. How has God acted in mercy so we might all be redeemed from sin and its consequences?

God mercifully resolved from all eternity to redeem the lives of each of us through Jesus Christ, who reveals the loving purposes of God.

a. John 1:3–5. What has come into being in him was life, and the life was the light of all people. The light shines in the darkness and the darkness did not overcome it.

b. Matt. 4:16. The people who sat in darkness have seen a great light, and for those who sat in the region and shadow of death light has dawned.

c. John 6:51. "I am the living bread that came down from heaven. Whoever eats of this bread will live forever; and the bread that I will give for the life of the world is my flesh."

Cf. Matt. 11:25–30; Mark 5:21–43; Isa. 9:2.

54. How did God prepare humankind for the coming of the Savior?

God prepared humankind for the coming of the Savior by the love and promises with which God guided the people of Israel, and by the truth God entrusted to the biblical prophets.

a. Isa. 41:10. Do not fear, for I am with you, do not be afraid, for I am your God; I will strengthen you, I will help you, I will uphold you with my victorious right hand.

b. Jer. 33:15–16. In those days and at that time I will cause a righteous Branch to spring up from David; and he shall execute justice and righteousness in the land. In those days Judah will be saved and Jerusalem will live in safety. And this is the name by which it will be called: "The Lord is our righteousness."

c. Mic. 5:2. But you, O Bethlehem of Ephrathah, who are one of the little clans of Judah, from you shall come forth for me one who is to rule in Israel, whose origin is from of old, from ancient days.

d. Isa. 40:3–5. A voice cries out: "In the wilderness prepare the way of the Lord, make straight in the desert a highway for our God. Every valley shall be lifted up, and every mountain and hill be made low; the uneven ground shall become level, and the rough places a plain. Then the glory of the Lord shall be revealed, and all people shall see it together, for the mouth of the Lord has spoken."

e. Isa. 9:6. For a child has been born for us, a son given to us; authority rests upon his shoulders; and he is named Wonderful Counselor, Mighty God, Everlasting Father, Prince of Peace.

f. Acts 10:43. "All the prophets testify about him that everyone who believes in him receives forgiveness of sins through his name."

Cf. Luke 4:14–21; Isa. 43:14–21.

THE SECOND ARTICLE
OF THE CHRISTIAN FAITH

55. What is the Second Article of the Christian Faith?

I believe in Jesus Christ, his only Son, our Lord, who was conceived by the Holy Spirit, born of the Virgin Mary, suffered under Pontius Pilate, was crucified, died, and was buried; he descended into hell. On the third day he rose again; he ascended into heaven and is seated at the right hand of God, the Father almighty, from where he will come to judge the living and the dead.

56. What does the Second Article of the Christian Faith confess?

The Second Article confesses faith in Jesus Christ, the Son of God, and the work of redemption.

57. Who is Jesus Christ?

Jesus Christ is truly divine and truly human in one person, my Savior, Redeemer, and Lord.

a. Isa. 48:16–17. Draw near to me, hear this! From the beginning I have not spoken in secret, from the time it came to be I have been there. And now the Lord God has sent me and his spirit. Thus says the Lord, your Redeemer, . . . who teaches you for your own good, who leads you in the way you should go.

b. Luke 2:10–11. The angel said to them, "Do not be afraid; for see — I am bringing you good news of great joy for all the people: to you is born this day in the city of David a Savior, who is the Messiah, the Lord."

Cf. Luke 1:67–79.

58. How does the Bible proclaim that Jesus Christ is truly God?

The Bible proclaims that in Jesus Christ the eternal word of God was made flesh and lived among us full of grace and truth. God's nature, as holy love, though seemingly hidden to the world in weakness, is fully made known. The Bible declares the good news that God is in Christ bringing reconciliation to the world and drawing all creation, including the poor and those who live at the margins of society, close to the loving heart of God.

a. Phil. 2:5–7. Let the same mind be in you that was in Christ Jesus, who, though he was in the form of God, did not regard equality with God as something to be exploited, but emptied himself, taking the form of a slave, being born in human likeness.

b. Col. 2:8–9. See to it that no one takes you captive through philosophy and empty deceit, according to human tradition, . . . and not according to Christ. For in him the whole fullness of deity dwells bodily.

c. 1 Cor. 13:13. Faith, hope, and love abide, these three; and the greatest of these is love.

Cf. Luke 2:25–32.

59. How does the Bible proclaim that the Son of God became truly human?

The Bible proclaims that Jesus Christ was conceived by the Holy Spirit and was born of the Virgin Mary. He became one of us, truly human in all things as we are, yet without sin.

a. Luke 1:35. The angel said to her, "The Holy Spirit will come upon you, and the power of the Most High will overshadow you; therefore the child to be born will be holy; he will be called Son of God."

b. John 1:14. And the Word became flesh and lived among us, and we have seen his glory, the glory as of a father's only son, full of grace and truth.

Cf. Luke 1:46–55; Matt. 1:18–25; Mark 6:1–4.

60. How did Christ reveal himself as the Savior before his passion and the crucifixion?

Christ revealed himself as the Savior before his passion and the crucifixion by his life, which was filled with love for the world around him, including those who lived at the margins of society. His teaching and his proclamation of the forgiveness of sins through faith in him, and also the miracles he performed, reveal his being God's Son, the Savior of the whole creation.

a. Mark 6:34. He saw a great crowd, and he had compassion for them, because they were like sheep without a shepherd; and he began to teach them many things.

b. Matt. 14:14. He saw a great crowd; and he had compassion for them and cured their sick.

c. Matt. 14:35–36. After the people of that place recognized him, they sent word throughout the region and brought all who were sick to him, and begged him that they might touch even the fringe of his cloak; and all who touched it were healed.

Cf. Luke 19:1–10; John 13:3–17; Matt. 25:31–40; Luke 9:10–17.

61. How did Christ accomplish our redemption?

Christ accomplished our redemption by his suffering and death upon the cross. He took upon himself our sin and carried it to the cross where it was crucified with him. In other words, God in compassion reaches out to us, steps into our distress, and makes it completely God's own.

a. Isa. 53:4–5. Surely he has borne our infirmities and cured our diseases; yet we accounted him stricken, struck down by God, and afflicted. But he was wounded for our transgressions, crushed for our iniquities, upon him was the punishment that made us whole, and by his bruises we are healed.

b. 2 Cor. 5:19. In Christ God was reconciling the world to himself, not counting their trespasses against them, and entrusting the message of reconciliation to us.

c. 2 Cor. 5:21. For our sake he made him to be sin who knew no sin, so that in him we might become the righteousness of God.

d. 1 John 3:16. We know love by this, that he laid down his life for us — and we ought to lay down our lives for one another.

e. 1 John 4:10. In this is love, not that we loved God but that he loved us and sent his Son to be the atoning sacrifice for our sins.

Cf. Rom. 5:1–5; Eph. 3:14–21.

62. Why was the death of Christ necessary for our redemption?

The death of Christ was necessary because we could be redeemed neither by teaching nor by example, but only by the loving sacrifice and self-giving of our Lord Jesus Christ on the cross.

a. John 15:13. No one has greater love than this, to lay down one's life for one's friends.

b. 1 Cor. 1:23–25. We proclaim Christ crucified, a stumbling block to Jews and foolishness to Gentiles, but to those who are the called, both Jews and Greeks, Christ the power of God and the wisdom of God. For God's foolishness is wiser than human wisdom, and God's weakness is stronger than human strength.

Cf. Mark 15.

63. Of what importance is Christ's burial?

Christ's burial is testimony to the fact that he really died. It shows that God in Christ has made the plight of humanity completely God's own.

a. Rom. 6:23. The wages of sin is death, but the free gift of
   God is eternal life in Christ Jesus our Lord.

   Cf. Mark 15:42–47.

64. What is meant when we say, "He descended into hell"?

This statement means that Jesus went to the place of departed
spirits to bring them hope, the message of salvation. When we
confess this we are saying that Jesus endures the plight that
ought to be ours and proclaims the Gospel even to those in
deepest despair. Christ's descent into hell reveals the complete
self-surrender of God out of love for us all.

a. 1 Pet. 3:18–20. For Christ also suffered for sins once for
   all, the righteous for the unrighteous, in order to bring you
   to God. He was put to death in the flesh, but made alive in
   the spirit, in which also he went and made a proclamation
   to the spirits in prison, who in former times did not obey,
   when God waited patiently in the days of Noah, during the
   building of the ark, in which a few, that is, eight persons,
   were saved through water.

b. Col. 1:13–14. He has rescued us from the power of darkness and transferred us into the kingdom of his beloved
   Son, in whom we have redemption, the forgiveness of sins.

65. What is meant when we say that Jesus Christ rose again from the dead?

When we confess this we are saying that the resurrection
proves Jesus to be the Son of God; that he is our Redeemer, in
whom we have new life, and that we also shall be raised from
the dead. We confess that by the grace of God there is an empty
grave; that the new life proclaimed in Christ is not merely a
hope, but an event in which we can all share and be glad.

a. Rom. 8:11. If the Spirit of him who raised Jesus from the dead dwells in you, he who raised Christ from the dead will give life to your mortal bodies also through his Spirit that dwells in you.

b. Rom. 6:4. Therefore we have been buried with him by baptism into death, so that, just as Christ was raised from the dead by the glory of the Father, so we too might walk in newness of life.

c. John 11:25–26. "I am the resurrection and the life. Those who believe in me, even though they die, will live, and everyone who lives and believes in me will never die."

Cf. Matt. 28:1–15.

66. What does it mean when we say that Christ ascended into heaven?

When we confess this we are saying that forty days after his resurrection, Christ was visibly taken into heaven, there to prepare a place for us. As Scripture declares, the Lord, the lover of justice and peace, "is exalted over all the peoples" (Ps. 99:2).

a. Ps. 97:9. You, O Lord, are most high over all the earth; you are exalted far above all gods.

b. John 17:24. "Father, I desire that those also, whom you have given me, may be with me where I am, to see my glory, which you have given me because you loved me before the foundation of the world."

c. John 14:1–3. "Do not let your hearts be troubled. Believe in God, believe also in me. In my Father's house there are many dwelling places. If it were not so, would I have told you that I go to prepare a place for you? And if I go and prepare a place for you, I will come again and will take you to myself, so that where I am, there you may be also."

Cf. Acts 1:1–11.

67. What does it mean when we say, "He is seated at the right hand of God the Father almighty"?

When we confess this we are saying that the risen and ascended Christ is in heaven in the full power and glory of God. As Scripture declares: "O sing to the Lord a new song, for he has done marvelous things" (Ps. 98:1).

a. Col. 3:1. So if you have been raised with Christ, seek the things that are above, where Christ is, seated at the right hand of God.

b. Rom. 8:33–34. Who will bring any charge against God's elect? It is God who justifies. Who is to condemn? It is Christ Jesus, who died, yes, who was raised, who is at the right hand of God, who indeed intercedes for us.

Cf. Eph. 1:20–23.

68. What does it mean when we say, "From where he will come to judge the living and the dead"?

When we confess this we are saying that Christ will come to us at the end of time with great power and glory, and that his judgment will be pronounced on the living and the dead, that is, on all who have ever lived and died. As Scripture declares: "Let the heavens be glad, and let the earth rejoice"; let all creation clap its hands. "He will judge the world with righteousness, and the peoples with his truth" (Ps. 96:11, 13).

a. Rom. 15:13. May the God of hope fill you with all joy and peace in believing, so that you may abound in hope by the power of the Holy Spirit.

b. Matt. 25:31–32. "When the Son of Man comes in his glory, and all the angels with him, then he will sit on the throne of his glory. All the nations will be gathered before him, and he will separate people one from another as a shepherd separates the sheep from the goats."

c. Luke 21:27–28. "Then they will see 'the Son of Man coming in a cloud' with power and great glory. Now when these things begin to take place, stand up and raise your heads, because your redemption is drawing near."

Cf. Matt. 25:34–45.

69. Where in the Holy Scripture do we find both the humble nature of Christ and the exaltation of our Savior briefly described?

We find the humble nature and the exaltation of Christ briefly described in Philippians 2:5–11. "Let the same mind be in you that was in Christ Jesus, who, though he was in the form of God, did not regard equality with God as something to be exploited, but emptied himself, taking the form of a slave, being born in human likeness. And being found in human form, he humbled himself and became obedient to the point of death — even death on a cross. Therefore, God also highly exalted him and gave him the name that is above every name, so that at the name of Jesus every knee should bend, in heaven and on earth and under the earth, and every tongue should confess that Jesus Christ is Lord, to the glory of God the Father."

70. What does the Church confess by this?

The Church confesses that every generation is summoned to live according to the pattern of Christ, close to the cross of Jesus and in the light of his resurrection. This means living thankfully, generously, and boldly in the midst of the suffering and turmoil of the world, as well as alongside its beauty and wonders, always rejoicing in the power of the Holy Spirit.

a. 1 Cor. 3:11. For no one can lay any foundation other than the one that has been laid; that foundation is Jesus Christ.

Cf. Mark 6:53–56; Mark 7:31–37; Matt. 10:16–31.

71. In summary, then, what does the Church believe about Jesus Christ?

The Church believes that Jesus Christ — true God, begotten of the Father from eternity, and also true man, born of the Virgin Mary — is our Lord.

72. What did Christ do for you?

I believe that he has redeemed, purchased, and delivered me, a lost and condemned creature, from all sins, from death, and from the power of evil.

73. How did he redeem you?

I believe that he has done this not with silver or gold, but with his holy, precious blood, and with his innocent suffering and death.

74. To what purpose did he redeem you?

I believe he has done this in order that I may belong to him, live under him in his kingdom, and serve him in eternal righteousness, innocence, and blessedness, just as he is risen from the dead and lives and rules eternally.

THE THIRD ARTICLE
OF THE CHRISTIAN FAITH

75. What is the Third Article of the Christian Faith?

I believe in the Holy Spirit, the one holy universal Christian Church, the communion of saints, the forgiveness of sins, the resurrection of the body, and the life everlasting.

76. What does the Third Article of the Christian Faith confess?

The Third Article confesses faith in the Holy Spirit and the godly life that the Spirit makes possible.

77. What does the Church believe about the Holy Spirit?

The Church believes that the Holy Spirit is the third person in the Holy Trinity, with the Father and the Son, true and eternal God, the distributor of all gifts, who enables us to come to Christ, our Lord, and to serve him in joy and discipleship, remaining with him forever.

78. How does the Holy Spirit inspire faith and discipleship among us?

The Holy Spirit works through the Word of God and the Holy Sacraments, which are the means of grace.

a. Ps. 25:4–5. Make me to know your ways, O Lord; teach me your paths. Lead me in your truth, and teach me, for you are the God of my salvation.

b. John 14:26. "But the Advocate, the Holy Spirit, whom the Father will send in my name, will teach you everything, and remind you of all that I have said to you."

c. Acts 1:8. "But you will receive power when the Holy Spirit has come upon you, and you will be my witnesses."
   Cf. Mark 14:22–25.

79. How does the Holy Spirit lead us to Christ?

The Holy Spirit makes known to us the call of God to come to Christ and follow him in humble, joyful discipleship. The Holy Spirit leads us by repentance and faith to the cross, instructing us in the meaning of faith, hope, and love, and enabling us to live the new life of the children of God.

a. Rom. 12:1–2. I appeal to you therefore, brothers and sisters, by the mercies of God, to present your bodies as a living sacrifice, holy and acceptable to God, which is your spiritual worship. Do not be conformed to this world, but be transformed by the renewing of your minds, so that you may discern what is the will of God — what is good and acceptable and perfect.

b. John 16:13–14. "When the Spirit of truth comes, he will guide you into all the truth.... He will glorify me, because he will take what is mine and declare it to you."

c. Rom. 12:12. Rejoice in hope, be patient in suffering, persevere in prayer.

Cf. Matt. 10:40–42.

80. What is faith?

Faith is complete trust in God and willing acceptance of God's grace in Jesus Christ.

a. Heb. 11:1. Now faith is the assurance of things hoped for, the conviction of things not seen.

b. Ps. 51:10–12. Create in me a clean heart, O God, and put a new and right spirit within me. Do not cast me away from your presence, and do not take your holy spirit from me. Restore to me the joy of your salvation, and sustain in me a willing spirit.

c. Rom. 1:17. It is written, "The one who is righteous will live by faith."

d. Ps. 143:10. Teach me to do your will, for you are my God. Let your good spirit lead me on a level path.

Cf. Rom. 3:21–31; Mark 4:35–41; Luke 7:1–10.

81. What is hope?

Hope is the gentle yet firm, unshakable conviction that God in Christ is radically committed to the world and all its people and wills that we should live reconciled one to another. It is even more. It is Scripture's assurance of a new heaven and a new earth, waiting for a day that is coming when we shall truly be what we already are in Christ, righteous in the eyes of God.

a. John 3:16. "For God so loved the world that he gave his only Son, so that everyone who believes in him may not perish but may have eternal life."

b. Ps. 62:5–6. For God alone my soul waits in silence, for my hope is from him. He alone is my rock and my salvation, my fortress; I shall not be shaken.

c. Ps. 130:5–6. I wait for the Lord, my soul waits, and in his word I hope; my soul waits for the Lord more than those who watch for the morning.

Cf. Rom. 5:1–11; Mark 9:14–29.

82. What is love?

Love is the way of God to us in Jesus Christ. It is reflected among people of faith as the Holy Spirit inspires the words and deeds of the Church in joyous, yet costly, discipleship.

a. Ps. 25:6. Be mindful of your mercy, O Lord, and of your steadfast love, for they have been from of old.

b. Ps. 33:4–5. The word of the Lord is upright, and all his work is done in faithfulness. He loves righteousness and justice; the earth is full of the steadfast love of the Lord.

c. John 13:34–35. "I give you a new commandment, that you love one another. Just as I have loved you, you also should love one another. By this everyone will know that you are my disciples, if you have love for one another."

Cf. Rom. 8:31–39; Mark 3:7–11.

83. What is sin?

Sin is unbelief and disobedience in thought and desire, word and deed, whereby evil is done or good is neglected, whether thoughtlessly or willfully.

a. Matt. 15:18. What comes out of the mouth proceeds from the heart, and this is what defiles.

b. Jas. 4:17. Anyone, then, who knows the right thing to do and fails to do it, commits sin.

Cf. Mark 12:1–11; Mark 14:12–50.

84. What is repentance?

Repentance is evidence of faith that is humbled. It consists of conviction of sin and sorrow for it, confession of sin and longing for grace. It is invariably accompanied by hope and by love.

a. Ps. 51:17. The sacrifice acceptable to God is a broken spirit; a broken and contrite heart, O God, you will not despise.

b. Matt. 5:6. "Blessed are those who hunger and thirst for righteousness, for they will be filled."

Cf. Luke 15:18–19; 2 Pet. 3:8–9.

85. How does the Bible speak of the change that takes place in our lives as a result of faith and repentance?

The Bible speaks of this change as being born anew. This is the new life into which we enter at the time of our baptism. It is a gift of God to us, inspired by the Holy Spirit.

a. John 3:3. "Very truly, I tell you, no one can see the kingdom of God without being born from above."

b. John 3:5. "Very truly, I tell you, no one can enter the kingdom of God without being born of water and Spirit."

c. Gal. 3:27–28. As many of you as were baptized into Christ have clothed yourselves with Christ. There is no longer Jew or Greek, there is no longer slave or free, there is no longer male and female; for all of you are one in Christ Jesus.

d. 1 Pet. 1:23. You have been born anew, not of perishable but of imperishable seed, through the living and enduring word of God.

Cf. 1 Pet. 1:3–9; Hosea 11:1–9; 1 Cor. 13; 1 Pet. 2:1–10.

86. What does this mean?

It means living a new life of discipleship by the power of God's word and the sacrament of baptism. Entering into the new life means living life not on our own terms but in accord with the way of Christ. It is neither a feeling with which we dare toy, nor a hobby. Rather, it is adherence to Christ. New life in Christ reflects the Church's belief that God is not an "adornment" of the world, but is rather a "lever" applied to the world. It is life that can spring only from grace.

a. Luke 14:27. Whoever does not carry the cross and follow me cannot be my disciple.

Cf. Matt. 10; Mark 10:35–45.

87. Is there such a thing as "cheap grace"?

Yes. Cheap grace is the false belief, widely held, that God's love for us requires little or nothing of us. It is the unsound belief that, having become aware of the awesome reality of God's love for us and the whole creation, life can go on as if nothing has changed. Cheap grace is faith without expectation, without risk, without a sense of wonder. Where cheap grace is rampant, the living word of God in Christ is ignored and the new life to which we are summoned has become a sham.

a. Luke 14:11. "All who exalt themselves will be humbled, and those who humble themselves will be exalted."

Cf. Mark 10:17–22; Isa. 5:1–7; Acts 5:1–11.

88. Is there such a thing as "costly grace"?

Yes. Where grace is not costly, it is not grace. It is costly because it summons us to live in the light of the word of God and to follow the call of Christ wherever it may lead us. It is grace because it is the presence of the new life by which we are embraced with the promises of God. Costly grace brings us to the foot of the cross and to the margins of society. It listens for the cries of the oppressed and looks for the tears of God in the world. It understands human existence and the meaning of life always in the light of Easter.

a. John 1:17. The law indeed was given through Moses; grace and truth came through Jesus Christ.

Cf. Ps. 1:1–3; Acts 20:18–24.

89. What is meant by "Church" in the Apostles' Creed?

By the one holy universal Christian Church we mean the entire body of Christians who seek to live by faith.

a. Rom. 12:4–6. For as in one body we have many members, and not all the members have the same function, so we, who are many, are one body in Christ, and individually we are members one of another. We have gifts that differ according to the grace given to us.

b. 1 Cor. 12:12–13. For just as the body is one and has many members, and all the members of the body, though many, are one body, so it is with Christ. For in the one Spirit we were all baptized into one body — Jews or Greeks, slaves or free — and we were all made to drink of one Spirit.

Cf. Rom. 12; Mark 4:35–41; Mark 8:34–38.

90. Why is the Church called "one"?

The Christian Church is called "one" because "there is one body and one Spirit, . . . one Lord, one faith, one baptism, one God and Father of all, who is above all and through all and in all." Eager to maintain "the unity of the Spirit in the bond of peace," its members are called to humility, gentleness, and patience in which each bears with the other in love.

Cf. Eph. 4:1–7.

91. Why is the Church called "holy"?

The Church is called "holy" because the Holy Spirit works mightily in it by Word and Sacrament to the end that all its members honor God through lives of prayer, worship, praise, and thanksgiving.

a. 1 Pet. 2:9. But you are a chosen race, a royal priesthood, a holy nation, God's own people, in order that you may proclaim the mighty acts of him who called you out of darkness into his marvelous light.

b. Eph. 5:25–27. Christ loved the church and gave himself up for her, in order to make her holy by cleansing her with the washing of water by the word, so as to present the church to himself in splendor, without a spot or wrinkle or anything of the kind — yes, so that she may be holy and without blemish.

Cf. Phil. 4:4–7; Col. 1:3–20.

92. Why is the Church called "universal"?

The Church is called "universal" because God has meant it for all persons and because where the Gospel is proclaimed, all are welcome and included.

a. Matt. 11:28–30. "Come to me, all you that are weary and are carrying heavy burdens, and I will give you rest. Take my yoke upon you, and learn from me; for I am gentle and humble in heart, and you will find rest for your souls. For my yoke is easy, and my burden is light."

b. Mark 16:15. And he said to them, "Go into all the world and proclaim the good news to the whole creation."

Cf. Matt. 28:16–20.

93. Why is the Church called the "Christian" Church?

The Church is called "Christian" because Christ alone is its foundation, its head, its hope, its light, and its truth.

a. John 15:5. "I am the vine, you are the branches. Those who abide in me and I in them bear much fruit, because apart from me you can do nothing."

b. Eph. 4:15–16. Speaking the truth in love, we must grow up in every way into him who is the head, into Christ, from whom the whole body, joined and knit together by every ligament with which it is equipped, as each part is working properly, promotes the body's growth in building itself up in love.

c. Col. 1:17–20. He himself is before all things, and in him all things hold together. He is the head of the body, the church; . . . in him all the fullness of God was pleased to dwell, and through him God was pleased to reconcile to himself all things, . . . through the blood of his cross.

Cf. 1 Cor. 3.

94. What do we understand by the "communion of saints"?

By the "communion of saints" we understand the Church and all its members, the blessed ones who have gone before us, and those who shall come after us; all who believe, love, and hope in the graciousness of God and participate in the treasures entrusted to the Church. The communion of saints shall always be found under the cross.

a. Phil. 2:2–4. Make my joy complete: be of the same mind, having the same love, being in full accord and of one mind. Do nothing from selfish ambition or conceit, but in humility regard others as better than yourselves. Let each of you look not to your own interests, but to the interests of others.

b. Gal. 6:14. May I never boast of anything except the cross of our Lord Jesus Christ.

Cf. John: 19:25–30.

95. What is the mission of the Church?

The mission of the Church is to be free for humanity. The Church is to proclaim the kingdom of God in all its grace and power, celebrating the Gospel in the world in word and deed. As it does this it confesses the truth that God stands above all gods and requires not only decision, but practice and action.

a. Isa. 52:7. How beautiful upon the mountains are the feet of the messenger who announces peace, who brings good news, who announces salvation, who says to Zion, "Your God reigns."

b. Matt. 24:14. And this good news of the kingdom will be proclaimed throughout the world, as a testimony to all the nations.

c. John 8:31–32. "If you continue in my word, you are truly my disciples; and you will know the truth, and the truth will make you free."

d. Eph. 4:15. Speaking the truth in love, we must grow up in every way into him who is the head, into Christ.

Cf. Acts 2; Acts 3:1–10; Exod. 16:13–36; Matt. 15:32–39.

96. What is the kingdom of God?

The kingdom of God is the rule of God established in the hearts and lives of all who seek to live by faith in Jesus Christ. Where Christ is present the hungry are fed, the poor are embraced, walls of hostility come down, "the lion lives alongside the lamb."

a. Luke 17:20–21. "The kingdom of God is not coming with things that can be observed; nor will they say, 'Look, here it is!' or 'There it is!' For, in fact, the kingdom of God is among you."

b. Isa. 11:8–9. The nursing child shall play over the hole of the asp, and the weaned child shall put its hand on the adder's den. They will not hurt or destroy on all my holy mountain; for the earth will be full of the knowledge of the Lord as the waters cover the sea.

Cf. Matt. 13:44–46; Isa. 56:1–8; Mark 4:26–29; Matt. 9:10–13.

97. Where did Christ set forth the principles of the kingdom of God?

Christ set forth the principles of the kingdom of God in the Sermon on the Mount. At the heart of the Sermon on the Mount are the Beatitudes.

Cf. Matt. 5–7; Luke 6:20–49.

Blessed are the poor in spirit, for theirs is the kingdom of heaven.

Blessed are those who mourn, for they will be comforted.

Blessed are the meek, for they will inherit the earth.

Blessed are those who hunger and thirst for righteousness, for they will be filled.

Blessed are the merciful, for they will receive mercy.

Blessed are the pure in heart, for they will see God.

Blessed are the peacemakers, for they will be called children of God.

Blessed are those who are persecuted for righteousness' sake, for theirs is the kingdom of heaven.

Blessed are you when people revile you and utter all kinds of evil against you falsely on my account. Rejoice and be glad, for your reward is great in heaven, for in the same way they persecuted the prophets who were before you.

Cf. Matt. 5:3–12; Luke 6:20–23; 1 Kings 3:3–14.

98. What is meant by the words "I believe in the forgiveness of sins"?

"I believe in the forgiveness of sins" means that God's grace is present in Christ for all humankind and is evidence of the

mercy of God. It is the truth of which the angels sing, the love
that embraced the prodigal son and caused the woman at the
well, in surprise and wonder, to rejoice with hope.

a. Luke 15:21–24. "Father, I have sinned against heaven and
   before you; I am no longer worthy to be called your son."
   But the father said to his slaves, "Quickly, bring out a
   robe — the best one — and put it on him; put a ring on his
   finger and sandals on his feet. And get the fatted calf and
   kill it, and let us eat and celebrate; for this son of mine
   was dead and is alive again, he was lost and is found!"
   And they began to celebrate.

   Cf. Luke 15:11–32; John 4:1–30; Luke 19:1–10.

99. What do we understand by "the resurrection of the body"?

By "the resurrection of the body" the Church confesses that,
by the grace of God, our lives do not end in death. Rather, we
live in hope and with the astonishing promise that God intends
to bring us out of darkness into his marvelous and eternal light
at the end of time. Thus we live in joyful anticipation of the
day of resurrection when Christ will raise us up with all who
have died.

a. 1 Cor. 15:42–44. So it is with the resurrection of the dead.
   What is sown is perishable, what is raised is imperishable.
   It is sown in dishonor, it is raised in glory. It is sown in
   weakness, it is raised in power. It is sown a physical body,
   it is raised a spiritual body.

b. 1 Cor. 15:54–58. "Death has been swallowed up in
   victory." "Where, O death, is your victory? Where,
   O death, is your sting?" The sting of death is sin, and the
   power of sin is the law. But thanks be to God, who gives
   us the victory through our Lord Jesus Christ. Therefore,

my beloved, be steadfast, immovable, always excelling in the work of the Lord, because you know that in the Lord your labor is not in vain.

Cf. 1 Cor. 15; Phil. 3:20–21.

100. What does the Church confess when it proclaims "the life everlasting"?

By "the life everlasting" the Church confesses that in the resurrection all children of God shall receive the glory of Christ in body and soul and shall abide with him forever.

a. 1 Cor. 13:12. For now we see in a mirror, dimly, but then we will see face to face. Now I know only in part; then I will know fully, even as I have been fully known.

b. Matt. 25:34. "Come, you that are blessed by my Father, inherit the kingdom prepared for you from the foundation of the world."

c. Rev. 21:3–4. "See, the home of God is among mortals. He will dwell with them as their God; they will be his peoples, and God himself will be with them; he will wipe every tear from their eyes. Death will be no more; mourning and crying and pain will be no more, for the first things have passed away."

Cf. John 14:1–7; Gen. 50:15–21; Rom. 8:28–39.

A SUMMARY OF THE THIRD ARTICLE OF THE CHRISTIAN FAITH

101. How does one become a Christian?

I believe that I cannot by my own reason or strength believe in Jesus Christ my Lord or come to him, but instead the Holy Spirit has called me through the Gospel, enlightened me with his gifts, made me holy, and kept me in the true faith.

102. In what way does the Holy Spirit work?

The Holy Spirit calls, gathers, enlightens, and makes holy the whole Christian Church on earth and keeps it with Jesus Christ in the one true faith.

103. What do you receive in the Church through the Holy Spirit?

In the Christian Church the Holy Spirit daily and abundantly forgives all sins, mine and those of all believers.

104. What is your hope for the future?

My hope is that on the last day Christ will raise me and all the dead and will give to me and all believers everlasting life. This is most certainly true.

Part IV

Prayer

105. What is prayer?

Prayer is the conversation of the heart with God for the purpose of praising God, asking God to supply our needs and those of others, and thanking God for all God gives us. Prayer is a sigh. It is sometimes speechless. It can be subversive. It is unafraid to lift its voice amid the pyramids of indifference and the vast deserts of conformity to evil that take our breath away.

a. Ps. 19:14. Let the words of my mouth and the meditation of my heart be acceptable to you, O Lord, my rock and my redeemer.

b. Ps. 34:3. O magnify the Lord with me, and let us exalt his name together.

c. Matt. 7:7–8. "Ask, and it will be given you; search, and you will find; knock, and the door will be opened for you. For everyone who asks receives, and everyone who searches finds, and for everyone who knocks, the door will be opened."

d. Ps. 92:1–2. It is good to give thanks to the Lord, to sing praises to your name, O Most High; to declare your steadfast love in the morning, and your faithfulness by night.

e. Ps. 130:1–2. Out of the depths I cry to you, O Lord. Lord, hear my voice!

Cf. Mark 14:32–42.

106. In what prayer has the Lord Jesus taught us how to pray?

Jesus taught us to pray by giving us the Lord's Prayer: "Our Father in heaven, hallowed be your name. Your kingdom come, your will be done, on earth as it is in heaven. Give us this day our daily bread, and forgive us our debts, as we forgive our debtors; and lead us not into temptation, but deliver us from evil, for yours is the kingdom, and the power, and the glory forever."

Cf. Matt. 6:9–13; Luke 11:2–4.

107. What do we mean when we say, "Our Father in heaven"?

Our heavenly Father desires us and all the children of God to pray with cheerful confidence, as beloved children look to a kind, loving father or mother, knowing that God is both willing and able to help us.

a. Matt. 7:9–11. "Is there anyone among you who, if your child asks for bread, will give a stone? Or if the child asks for a fish, will give a snake? If you then, who are evil, know how to give good gifts to your children, how much more will your Father in heaven give good things to those who ask him!"

b. John 16:27. "For the Father himself loves you, because you have loved me and have believed that I came from God."

c. Ps. 121:1–2. I lift up my eyes to the hills — from where will my help come? My help comes from the Lord, who made heaven and earth.

108. What do we mean when we say, "Hallowed be your name"?

We pray that God's name may be kept holy among us as it is holy in itself. This is done when the Word of God is truthfully taught and we as the children of God seek to live lives of faith, joy, and gratitude in accord with God's Word.

a. 1 Sam. 2:2. "There is no Holy One like the Lord, no one besides you; there is no Rock like our God."

b. Ps. 72:18–19. Blessed be the Lord, the God of Israel, who alone does wondrous things. Blessed be his glorious name forever; may his glory fill the whole earth.

c. Matt. 5:16. "Let your light shine before others, so that they may see your good works and give glory to your Father in heaven."

109. What do we mean when we say, "Your kingdom come"?

We pray that we and all others may share in the kingdom of God, which is established by the grace of God in Jesus Christ, and that its rule may govern our hearts and be extended throughout all the world.

a. Ps. 85:10–11. Steadfast love and faithfulness will meet; righteousness and peace will kiss each other. Faithfulness will spring up from the ground, and righteousness will look down from the sky.

b. Rev. 11:15. "The kingdom of the world has become the kingdom of our Lord and of his Messiah, and he will reign forever and ever."

110. What do we mean when we say, "Your will be done, on earth as it is in heaven"?

We pray that God's good and gracious will may be done by us and all others as cheerfully as it is done by the angels in heaven.

a. Heb. 13:20–21. Now may the God of peace...make you complete in everything good so that you may do his will, working among us that which is pleasing in his sight, through Jesus Christ, to whom be the glory forever and ever.

b. Rom. 12:2. Do not be conformed to this world, but be transformed by the renewing of your minds, so that you may discern what is the will of God — what is good and acceptable and perfect.

111. What do we mean when we say, "Give us this day our daily bread"?

We pray that as we look to God to supply the needs of our bodies and our souls, God will make us truly thankful for these gifts.

a. Ps. 34:8. O taste and see that the Lord is good; happy are those who take refuge in him.

b. Ps. 30:10. Hear, O Lord, and be gracious to me! O Lord, be my helper!

c. Ps. 145:15–16. The eyes of all look to you, and you give them their food in due season. You open your hand, satisfying the desire of every living thing.

d. Ps. 6:2. Be gracious to me, O Lord, for I am languishing; O Lord, heal me, for my bones are shaking with terror.

e. Ps. 67:1. May God be gracious to us and bless us and make his face to shine upon us.

112. What do we mean when we say, "Forgive us our debts,
as we forgive our debtors"?

We pray that God will graciously forgive our sin and we ask that we might have the willingness and strength to forgive others.

a. Ps. 51:1–2. Have mercy on me, O God, according to your steadfast love; according to your abundant mercy blot out my transgressions. Wash me thoroughly from my iniquity, and cleanse me from my sin.

b. Matt. 6:14–15. "If you forgive others their trespasses, your heavenly Father will also forgive you; but if you do not forgive others, neither will your Father forgive your trespasses."

c. Matt. 18:21–22. Then Peter came and said to him, "Lord, if another member of the church sins against me, how often should I forgive? As many as seven times?" Jesus said to him, "Not seven times, but, I tell you, seventy-seven times."

113. What do we mean when we say, "Lead us not into temptation"?

We pray that God may protect us and renew our strength when we are tempted by the power of evil.

a. Isa. 40:31. Those who wait for the Lord shall renew their strength, they shall mount up with wings like eagles, they shall run and not be weary, they shall walk and not faint.

b. 1 Cor. 10:13. God is faithful, and he will not let you be tested beyond your strength, but with the testing he will also provide the way out so that you may be able to endure it.

114. What do we mean when we say, "But deliver us from evil"?

We pray that God may protect us from those thoughts, words, and deeds that deny our Lord Jesus Christ; give us the strength to resist the seductions of the world, including the false claims of the powers and principalities; and when our life on earth comes to an end, lovingly welcome us to eternal life.

a. Jer. 31:3. I have loved you with an everlasting love; therefore I have continued my faithfulness to you.

b. John 17:15. "I am not asking you to take them out of the world, but I ask you to protect them from the evil one."

c. 2 Tim. 4:18. The Lord will rescue me from every evil attack and save me for his heavenly kingdom. To him be the glory forever and ever.

115. How can a loving God permit so much evil in the world?

The catastrophes of nature and humankind silence our wisdom. Yet we believe, in the face of every contradiction of God's love in the fallen world, that God remains faithful to the divine promises, that grace and truth endure despite every assault, and that God not only shares the pain of sin in the world, but absorbs it in Jesus Christ, who calls us to resist the power of evil, embracing his passion and victory, while rejoicing in the power of the Holy Spirit. And so we are bold and able to confess with our forebears: "Christ is risen. He is risen indeed!"

116. What do we mean when we say, "For yours is the kingdom, and the power, and the glory forever"?

In these closing words of the Lord's Prayer we express our confidence that God hears our prayers and answers them. We confess our faith that God's kingdom, and power, and glory shall endure forever. And we say "Amen."

a. 2 Cor. 1:20. For in him, every one of God's promises is a "Yes." For this reason it is through him that we say the "Amen" to the glory of God.

b. Eph. 3:20–21. Now to him who by the power at work within us is able to accomplish abundantly far more than all we can ask or imagine, to him be glory in the church and in Christ Jesus to all generations, forever and ever. Amen.

117. Why is prayer necessary?

Prayer is necessary because it gives expression to the deepest longings of our hearts. It is evidence, as well, of grace at work among us, and the presence of the Holy Spirit in our lives and in the life of the Church. We are invited to pray and thus to be drawn toward God, who welcomes our prayers and promises to hear them.

a. Jer. 29:12–13. When you call upon me and come and pray to me, I will hear you. When you search for me, you will find me; if you seek me with all your heart.

b. Ps. 65:5. By awesome deeds you answer us with deliverance, O God of our salvation; you are the hope of all the ends of the earth and of the farthest seas.

c. Jas. 5:16. Pray for one another, so that you may be healed. The prayer of the righteous is powerful and effective.

118. How should we pray?

We should pray humbly because of our need and unworthiness. We should pray gratefully because of God's loving-kindness.

a. Dan. 9:18. We do not present our supplication before you on the ground of our righteousness, but on the ground of your great mercies.

b. John 15:7. If you abide in me, and my words abide in you, ask for whatever you wish, and it will be done for you.

c. Jas. 1:6. But ask in faith, never doubting, for the one who doubts is like a wave of the sea, driven and tossed by the wind.

119. Are all our prayers answered?

Yes. All our prayers are answered either in the way we expect God to answer them or in the way God knows will be best for us.

a. Ps. 40:1–2. I waited patiently for the Lord; he inclined to me and heard my cry. He drew me up from the desolate pit, out of the miry bog, and set my feet upon a rock.

b. Hab. 1:2. O Lord, how long shall I cry for help, and you will not listen?

c. Gen. 32:26. But Jacob said: "I will not let you go, unless you bless me."

d. Ps. 10:17–18. O Lord, you will hear the desire of the meek; you will strengthen their heart, you will incline your ear to do justice for the orphan and the oppressed.

e. Matt. 26:39. He threw himself on the ground and prayed, "My Father, if it is possible, let this cup pass from me; yet not what I want but what you want."

Part V

The Sacrament of Holy Baptism

120. What is a sacrament?

A sacrament is a sacred ordinance of the Church instituted by Jesus Christ in which by visible signs and means he imparts and preserves the new life.

Cf. Mark 14:17–25; Luke 22:14–20; John 13:1–20; Mark 1:4–11.

121. How many sacraments has Christ instituted?

Christ has instituted two sacraments, Holy Baptism and the Lord's Supper.

Cf. Matt. 3:11–17; Matt. 26:26–29.

122. With what words did Christ institute the sacrament of Holy Baptism?

Christ instituted the sacrament of Holy Baptism with these words: "All authority in heaven and on earth has been given to me. Go therefore and make disciples of all nations, baptizing them in the name of the Father and of the Son and of the Holy Spirit, and teaching them to obey everything that I have commanded you. And remember, I am with you always, to the end of the age."

Cf. Matt. 28:16–20.

123. What does God do for us in Holy Baptism?

In Holy Baptism God acts graciously toward us through the forgiveness of sins, trusts us with the gift of new life, receives us into the communion of saints as beloved children, welcomes us to the fellowship and discipleship of the Christian Church, and sends us into the world as witnesses to the Gospel in mission.

a. Rom. 6:3–4. Do you not know that all of us who have been baptized into Christ Jesus were baptized into his death? Therefore we have been buried with him by baptism into death, so that, just as Christ was raised from the dead by the glory of the Father, so we too might walk in newness of life.

Cf. Ps. 71:1–3.

124. What does Holy Baptism require of us?

Holy Baptism requires of us that by daily repentance and prayer we strip ourselves of all that separates us from God and our neighbor — our pride, our idolatries, our selfish desires — and embrace in faith the new life as God's gift.

a. Ps. 98:1. O sing to the Lord a new song, for he has done marvelous things.

b. Col. 3:9–10. Do not lie to one another, seeing that you have stripped off the old self with its practices and have clothed yourselves with the new self, which is being renewed in knowledge according to the image of its creator.

c. Ps. 147:7–8, 10–11. Sing to the Lord with thanksgiving; ... He covers the heavens with clouds, prepares rain for the earth, makes grass grow on the hills.... His delight is not in the strength of the horse, nor his pleasure in the speed of a runner; but the Lord takes pleasure in those who fear him, in those who hope in his steadfast love.

Cf. Rom. 12:9–21.

125. Why should little children be baptized?

Children should be baptized because the new life is a gift of God's love, which children need as much as adults, and are as able to receive as graciously as adults since the Lord Jesus has promised the kingdom of God to all, including children.

a. Acts 2:39. "For the promise is for you, for your children, and for all who are far away, everyone whom the Lord our God calls to him."

b. Mark 10:13–14, 16. People were bringing little children to him in order that he might touch them; and the disciples spoke sternly to them. But when Jesus saw this, he was indignant and said to them, "Let the little children come to me; do not stop them; for it is to such as these that the kingdom of God belongs...." And he took them up in his arms, laid his hands on them, and blessed them.

Cf. Mark 9:33–37.

126. What does the baptism of children require of parents and godparents?

Baptism requires that they help their children and godchildren to grow in the new life by Christian teaching and training and by prayer and example.

a. Matt. 5:16. "Let your light shine before others, so that they may see your good works and give glory to your Father in heaven."

b. Eph. 6:4. Do not provoke your children to anger, but bring them up in the discipline and instruction of the Lord.

Cf. John 13:12–15.

127. What is confirmation?

Confirmation is the renewal of promises made at the time of our baptism. It is daring to live life based on God's Word. Having been instructed in the basics of the Christian faith, we publicly confess faith in Jesus Christ, affirm the Gospel, and accept the tests, trials, and risks of living by faith.

a. Matt. 16:24. Jesus told his disciples, "If any want to become my followers, let them deny themselves and take up their cross and follow me."

b. John 13:20. "Very truly, I tell you, whoever receives one whom I send receives me; and whoever receives me receives him who sent me."

Cf. Matt. 10:40–42.

Part VI

The Sacrament of the Lord's Supper

128. What is the Lord's Supper (Holy Communion)?

The Lord's Supper (or Holy Communion) is the daily bread of the Church. It is the sacrament by which we receive the body and blood of our Lord Jesus Christ as the nourishment of our new life. In this sacrament we give thanks for the forgiveness of sins and the reality of grace. From the Lord's Table, each of us is sent into the world to live out our discipleship in Christ with all believers, confessing that he died for us, giving thanks and rejoicing that he lives and reigns among us.

a. 2 Cor. 5:17. So if anyone is in Christ, there is a new creation: everything old has passed away; see, everything has become new!

129. What are the visible signs and means of the sacrament of the Lord's Supper?

The visible signs and means of the sacrament of the Lord's Supper are bread and wine, partaken of by the communicant.

130. With what words did Christ institute the sacrament of the Lord's Supper (Holy Communion)?

The Lord Jesus on the night when he was betrayed took bread, and when he had given thanks, he broke it, and gave it to the disciples and said, "Take, eat; this is my body, which is for you. Do this in remembrance of me." In the same way also he took a cup, after supper, and when he had given thanks he gave it to them, saying, "Drink of it, all of you; for this is my blood of the covenant, which is poured out for many for the forgiveness of sins. Do this, as often as you drink it, in remembrance of me."

> Cf. Mark 14:22–24; Matt. 26:26–28; Luke 22:19–20;
> 1 Cor. 11:23–25.

131. What blessings do we receive as we eat and drink in the Lord's Supper?

As we eat and drink in the Lord's Supper we receive forgiveness of sins, new life, and salvation, as it is written: "My body broken, my blood shed for you for the remission of sins." We receive the blessings of this sacrament only as we eat and drink with heartfelt repentance and true faith in our Lord Jesus Christ.

a. John 6:51. "I am the living bread that came down from heaven. Whoever eats of this bread will live forever; and the bread that I will give for the life of the world is my flesh."

b. John 6:55–56. For my flesh is true food and my blood is true drink. Those who eat my flesh and drink my blood abide in me, and I in them.

c. 1 Cor. 10:17. Because there is one bread, we who are many are one body, for we all partake of the one bread.

d. 1 Cor. 11:26. For as often as you eat this bread and drink the cup, you proclaim the Lord's death until he comes.

e. Matt. 5:23–24. "So when you are offering your gift at the altar, if you remember that your brother or sister has something against you, leave your gift there before the altar and go; first be reconciled to your brother or sister, and then come and offer your gift."

132. What does our communion daily require of us?

Our communion requires that we daily keep in remembrance the crucifixion of our Lord Jesus, and that we consider well how hard it was for our Savior to bear our sins and the sins of the whole world, and to gain eternal salvation for us by offering up his life and shedding his blood. And since our sins caused the Lord Jesus the greatest sufferings, yea bitter death, we should have no pleasure in sin, but earnestly flee and avoid it; and being reclaimed by our Savior and Redeemer we should live, suffer, and die to his honor, so that at all times and especially in the hour of death we may cheerfully and confidently say:

Lord Jesus, for thee I live, for thee I suffer, for thee I die!
Lord Jesus, thine will I be in life and death!
Grant me, O Lord, eternal salvation!
Amen.

Selected Bibliography

Arndt, Elmer J. F., ed. *The Heritage of the Reformation.* New York: Richard E. Smith, Publisher, 1950.

Barth, Karl. *Evangelical Theology: An Introduction.* New York: Holt, Rinehart and Winston, 1963.

Bonhoeffer, Dietrich. *Life Together* and *Prayerbook of the Bible.* Dietrich Bonhoeffer Works 5. Minneapolis: Fortress Press, 1996.

Brown, Dale W. *Understanding Pietism.* Revised edition. Nappanee, Ind.: Evangel Publishing House, 1996.

Brueggemann, Walter. *The Evangelical Catechism Revisited, 1847–1972.* St. Louis: Eden Publishing House, 1972.

Busch, Eberhard. *Karl Barth and the Pietists.* Downers Grove, Ill.: InterVarsity Press, 2004.

Gelzer, David George. "Mission to America: A History of the Work of the Basel Foreign Missions Society in America." Doctoral dissertation, Yale University, 1952.

Hall, Douglas John. *The Cross in Our Context: Jesus and the Suffering World.* Minneapolis: Fortress Press, 2003.

Johnson, Elizabeth A. *Quest for the Living God: Mapping Frontiers in the Theology of God.* New York: Continuum, 2008.

Johnson, Maxwell E. *The Rites of Christian Initiation: Their Evolution and Interpretation.* Revised edition. Collegeville, Minn.: Liturgical Press, 2007.

Oberman, Heiko. *Luther.* New York: Doubleday, 1992.

Schneider, Carl E. *The German Church on the American Frontier.* St. Louis: Eden Publishing House, 1939; repr. Eugene, Ore., Wipf & Stock, 2009.

Soelle, Dorothee. *Suffering.* Philadelphia: Fortress Press, 1975.